## OECD ECONOMIC SURVEYS

# UNITED KINGDOM

## FEBRUARY 1983

### ORGANISATION FOR ECONOMIC CO-OPERATION AND DEVELOPMENT

Pursuant to article 1 of the Convention signed in Paris on 14th December, 1960, and which came into force on 30th September, 1961, the Organisation for Economic Co-operation and Development (OECD) shall promote policies designed:

- to achieve the highest sustainable economic growth and employment and a rising standard of living in Member countries, while maintaining financial stability, and thus to contribute to the development of the world economy;
- to contribute to sound economic expansion in Member as well as non-member countries in the process of economic development; and
- to contribute to the expansion of world trade on a multilateral, non-discriminatory basis in accordance with international obligations.

The Signatories of the Convention on the OECD are Austria, Belgium, Canada, Denmark, France, the Federal Republic of Germany, Greece, Iceland, Ireland, Italy, Luxembourg, the Netherlands, Norway, Portugal, Spain, Sweden, Switzerland, Turkey, the United Kingdom and the United States. The following countries acceded subsequently to this Convention (the dates are those on which the instruments of accession were deposited): Japan (28th April, 1964), Finland (28th January, 1969), Australia (7th June, 1971) and New Zealand (29th May, 1973).

The Socialist Federal Republic of Yugoslavia takes part in certain work of the OECD (agreement of 28th October, 1961).

# CONTENTS

## TABLES

# DIAGRAMS

# BASIC STATISTICS OF THE UNITED KINGDOM

## THE LAND

| | | | |
|---|---|---|---|
| Area (1 000 sq. km) | 244 | Major cities (population in millions, 1980 mid-year estimates): | |
| Agricultural area (1 000 sq. km), 1980 | 185 | Greater London | 6.8 |
| | | Birmingham | 1.0 |
| | | Glasgow | 0.8 |
| | | Liverpool | 0.5 |
| | | Manchester | 0.5 |

## THE PEOPLE

| | | | |
|---|---|---|---|
| Population (30.6.1981) | 56 020 000 | Total civilian employment, 1981 | 23 048 000 |
| No. inhabitants per sq. km | 230 | of which: | |
| Net increase in population, 1975-1980, annual average | −9 830 | Agriculture | 647 000 |
| | | Industry (incl. construction) | 8 375 000 |
| Percentage change at annual rates, 1975-1980 | 0.0 | Other activities | 14 076 000 |

## THE GOVERNMENT

| | | | |
|---|---|---|---|
| Public current expenditure 1981 (per cent of GNP) | 22 | Composition of House of Commons, November 1982 (No. of seats): | |
| Public sector current receipts 1981 (per cent of GNP) | 43 | Conservative | 333 |
| | | Labour | 237 |
| National debt 31st March 1981 (ratio to General Government revenue) | 119 | Social Democratic Party | 30 |
| | | Liberal | 12 |
| | | Northern Ireland Parties | 12 |
| | | Scottish National Party | 2 |
| | | Plaid Cymru | 2 |
| | | Independent Socialist | 1 |
| | | Vacant | 2 |
| | | Speaker | 1 |
| | | Other | 3 |
| | | | 635 |

Last general election: 3.5.1981

## FOREIGN TRADE

| | | | |
|---|---|---|---|
| Exports: | | Imports: | |
| Exports of goods and services as a percentage of the GNP (1981) | 27 | Imports of goods and services as a percentage of the GNP (1981) | 24 |
| Main exports (percentage of total exports in 1981): | | Main imports (percentage of total imports in 1981): | |
| Machinery | 23 | Machinery | 18 |
| Chemicals | 11 | Petroleum and petroleum products | 12 |
| Transport equipment | 10 | Chemicals | 7 |
| Chemicals | 11 | Non-ferrous metals | 3 |
| Textiles | 3 | Meat | 2 |
| Non-ferrous metals | 2 | | |
| Iron and steel | 2 | | |

## THE CURRENCY

| | | | |
|---|---|---|---|
| Monetary unit: Pound sterling | | Currency unit per US $, average of daily figures: | |
| | | Year 1981 | 0.4977 |
| | | November 1982 | 0.6131 |

*Note:* An international comparison of certain basic statistics is given in an annex table.

*This Survey is based on the Secretariat's study prepared for the annual review of the United Kingdom by the Economic and Development Review Committee on 16th December 1982.*

*After revisions in the light of discussions during the review, final approval of the Survey for publication was given by the Committee on 18th January 1983.*

# INTRODUCTION

The adjustment to the second oil shock, the tight stance of economic policy and the substantial loss of competitiveness have contributed to the deepest recession in the post-war period. The downturn was considerably stronger in the United Kingdom than generally elsewhere in the OECD area; real GDP declined by about 5 per cent in the three years to mid-1982 compared with a rise of 2 per cent in the OECD area as a whole. Labour market conditions have sharply deteriorated, in part influenced by exceptional counter-cyclical productivity growth. Employment declined substantially in the three years to mid-1982 while unemployment has more than doubled to a rate of about 12 per cent. The loss of output and employment in manufacturing has been particularly severe and there has been a considerable contraction of the industrial base. Reflecting the somewhat earlier onset of recession than in partner countries and the shift to being a net oil exporter in mid-1980, the current external account has been in sizeable surplus over the last two years, but more recently it has fallen considerably. These developments have been accompanied by a very sharp fall in the rate of inflation from a rate somewhat above the OECD average in 1981 to one among the lowest in the OECD area. With pay settlements falling, there seems to have been an important change in inflationary expectations and behaviour.

In conformity with the anti-inflationary objectives of the Medium-Term Financial Strategy, the Public Sector Borrowing Requirement has been considerably reduced and the monetary aggregates have developed close to the target range announced in the March 1982 Budget. The reduction in government borrowing together with trends in international financial markets has enabled the authorities to reduce sharply nominal interest rates. Nevertheless, with the success in bringing down inflation, real interest rates remain relatively high. The stance of fiscal policy although eased remains tight. In November 1982, the Government announced a further reduction in the national insurance surcharge and other measures in order to ease industry's costs. On the basis of current economic policies and exchange rates and with weak projected growth of world trade, the outlook up to mid-1984 is for only modest growth in real GDP, a further considerable rise in unemployment and a marked reduction in the current external surplus. The rate of inflation is projected to be further reduced.

This Survey commences with a review of recent developments in demand and output, the labour market, costs and prices and the balance of payments (Part I). Fiscal and monetary policies are discussed in Part II while Part III contains an analysis of short-term prospects up to mid-1984. Part IV examines the performance of manufacturing industry since 1973 and some aspects of the Government's micro-economic adjustment and industrial policies. The Survey concludes with a discussion of the main policy issues (Part V).

# I. RECENT DEVELOPMENTS

## Demand and output

The sharp turnaround in demand and output since 1979 is illustrated in Table 1. Most components of demand have fallen considerably for around two years but there has been some recovery in total domestic demand in the recent period. A notable feature has been the relative stability of private consumption during a period[1] when most components of real personal disposable income were falling. Real take-home pay[2] which rose at an average annual rate of about 4 per cent in the three years to 1980 fell by 1½ per cent in 1981 and has continued to decline in 1982 (Table 3). The increase in the tax burden rather than the slowdown in the growth of nominal earnings, was the main reason for this development. Self-employment income in real terms has also fallen

### Table 1. Demand and output
Percentage volume changes, seasonally adjusted at annual rate

|  | From previous year | | | | | From previous half year | | |
|---|---|---|---|---|---|---|---|---|
|  | 1978 | 1979 | 1980 | 1981 | 1982[1] | 1981 II | 1982 I | II[1] |
| Private consumption | 5.8 | 4.9 | −0.1 | 0.4 | 1 | −0.3 | 0.1 | 3½ |
| Government consumption | 2.1 | 1.8 | 1.9 | 0.0 | 1¾ | 1.6 | 1.3 | 2¾ |
| Fixed investment | 3.5 | 0.9 | −2.8 | −8.2 | 2½ | 1.3 | 4.1 | ¾ |
| Final domestic demand | 4.6 | 3.6 | −0.2 | −1.2 | 1¼ | 0.3 | 1.0 | 3 |
| *plus* stockbuilding[2] | −0.2 | 0.6 | −2.9 | −0.3 | 1 | 2.9 | 1.7 | −2 |
| *plus* compromise adjustment[2][3] | 0.1 | 0.3 | −0.3 | −0.2 | −¼ | 1.9 | −1.8 | ½ |
| Total domestic demand | 4.4 | 4.4 | −3.3 | −1.6 | 2 | 5.1 | 0.9 | 1½ |
| Exports | 1.9 | 2.6 | 0.4 | −2.2 | −¼ | 7.3 | −2.3 | −3 |
| Imports | 3.9 | 11.3 | −3.4 | −0.3 | 4¼ | 29.5 | −3.9 | −¾ |
| Change in foreign balance[2] | −0.6 | −2.4 | 1.1 | −0.5 | −1¼ | −5.7 | 0.6 | −½ |
| GDP at market prices[4] | 3.8 | 2.0 | −2.2 | −2.2 | ¾ | −0.8 | 1.5 | 1 |
| GDP m.p. excluding North Sea oil | 3.2 | 1.1 | −2.3 | −2.6 | ½ | −0.9 | 1.1 | ½ |
| Agricultural production | 7.8 | −0.1 | 9.6 | −0.8 | ¾ | 0.8 | 0.0 | 1½ |
| Mining and quarrying[5] | 24.6 | 27.5 | 1.8 | 6.2 | 9 | 4.4 | 10.2 | 10½ |
| Manufacturing | 0.6 | 0.1 | −9.1 | −6.4 | −¼ | 3.8 | −1.2 | −2½ |
| Construction, gas, electricity and water | 5.6 | −0.5 | −4.4 | −7.5 | ½ | 0.4 | −1.7 | 5 |
| Services | 3.0 | 1.9 | −0.7 | −0.7 | ½ | 0.1 | 0.1 | 2 |
| GDP at factor cost (on an output basis) | 3.3 | 2.0 | −2.9 | −2.4 | ½ | 1.3 | −0.1 | 1½ |
| Real personal disposable income | 8.2 | 6.9 | 1.3 | −1.9 | −2¼ | −3.0 | −2.3 | −1¼ |
| Personal savings rate | 12.7 | 14.4 | 15.6 | 13.4 | 10¾ | 12.8 | 11.8 | 9½ |

1. Estimation based on the Secretariat forecast of the fourth quarter 1982.
2. Contribution to GDP estimated by taking the change as a percentage of GDP in the previous period.
3. The difference between expenditure-based GDP and "compromise" GDP. The latter is the weighted average of the output, expenditure and income measure of GDP. The weights are respectively 40 per cent, 40 per cent and 20 per cent.
4. On a "compromise" basis.
5. Including North Sea oil and gas production.
*Sources: Economic Trends*, CSO and Secretariat estimates.

1. The percentage difference (actual rate) between the highest and lowest level of private consumption on a half-yearly basis between the first half of 1979 and the first half of 1982 was ¾ per cent.
2. Real disposable average earnings.

considerably. The impact of pay and self-employment income on real personal disposable income was moderated, however, by continuing strong growth of government transfers to households (6½ per cent a year on average), mainly social security payments, partly reflecting the rise in unemployment payments. As a result, real personal disposable income continued to rise in 1980, but at a markedly slower rate than in the previous two years before falling in 1981 and in 1982.

*Diagram 1.* **Investment trends**
Fixed investment at 1975 prices s.a. as a percent of GDP

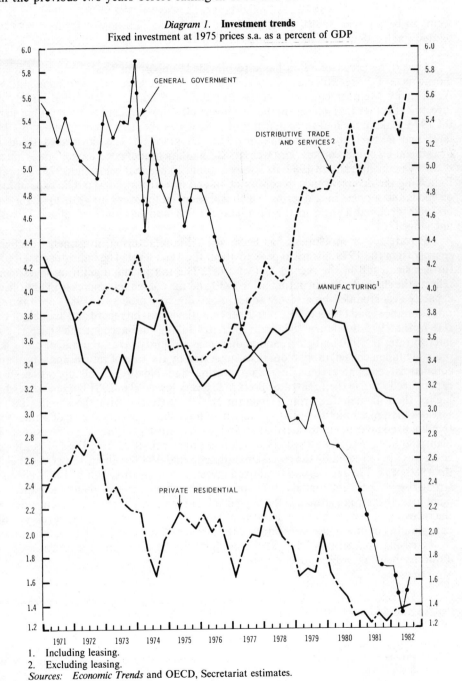

1. Including leasing.
2. Excluding leasing.
*Sources: Economic Trends* and OECD, Secretariat estimates.

The effect on private consumption of the fall in real personal disposable income was largely absorbed by changes in the saving ratio. After reaching an historical peak of 15½ per cent in 1980, the personal saving ratio has fallen progressively (Table 1) to about 12 per cent in the first half of 1982. Reflecting mainly the abolition of hire purchase controls in July – which stimulated a strong rise in private consumption – the saving ratio fell further in the third quarter to 9½ per cent, which is significantly below the average level in the 1970s. An important factor accounting for the fall of the ratio seems to be the real wealth effect produced by the deceleration of inflation and the related smaller decline in the real value of monetary assets, thus leading people to save less.

Government consumption has also provided support for final domestic demand during most of the recession despite cash limits and strict control on government outlays. As in many Member countries, curbs on public expenditure have fallen largely on investment rather than on consumption. Government investment has been falling since the 1973 peak: in the first three quarters of 1982 it was about 19 per cent below its 1981 level and 60 per cent lower than in 1973 (Diagram 1). The downward trend in investment by public corporations was less strong than that of government but despite a recovery in the first half of 1982, its level was some 20 per cent below the 1975/76 peak. Reflecting the diverse trends in consumption and investment, total public expenditure on goods and services in real terms, which had been flat for over four years up to the end of 1980, declined a little in the first half of 1981 and has since remained broadly unchanged.

Private sector investment has been weak. Manufacturing investment[3] declined sharply from the 1979 historical peak to about the 1965 level. The indicators point to a further small fall in the second half of 1982. The fall in manufacturing investment reflects the sharp decline in output after 1980 and the consequent increase in unutilised capacity accompanied by a severe squeeze on company profits. In 1981, pre-tax real rates of return[4] had fallen to just over 2 per cent, the lowest on record and about half the rate in the 1975 downturn (Diagram 2). After taking into account the sharp rise in interest rates in 1980 and 1981, and higher local authority taxes, the rate of profit has probably fallen considerably more than suggested by the rate of return. Industrial and commercial companies outside manufacturing and North Sea oil operations also experienced a fall in their real rate of return to a very low level in 1981 but one somewhat higher than in manufacturing (Diagram 2). This together with the smaller fall in services than manufacturing output may help to explain the persistence of an upward trend in fixed investment in distribution and services through 1982. Total investment in plant and machinery by all sectors which had grown rapidly during the 1970s (36 per cent) was also affected by the recession, falling in mid-1982 to about 10 per cent below the 1980 peak. The recovery in total fixed investment in the first half of 1982 reflects a strong rise (12 per cent annual rate) in private sector housing investment; the indicators point to further strong growth in the second half of the year. The principal factors behind the recovery in private housing investment from the extremely low 1981 level[5] are the near stability of new house prices during the last year, ample availability of finance due to increasing competition from banks, falling interest rates and reductions in local authority housing programmes.

3. The OECD figures on manufacturing investment include leasing, whereas official United Kingdom statistics exclude leasing because they classify investment by ownership. Manufacturing investment accounted for about 38 per cent of total industrial investment in 1981.

4. These rates relate to the rate of return on physical assets regardless of how they are financed; i.e. they include net interest payments.

5. Private housing in 1981 was 30 per cent below the 1979 level and nearly 40 per cent below the average of the 1970s.

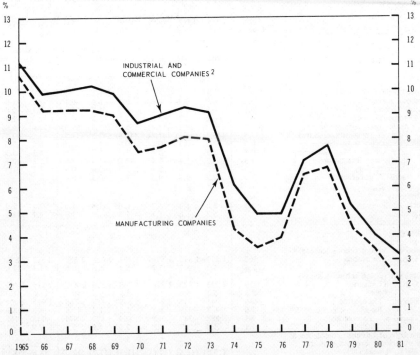

*Diagram 2.* **Real rates of return in industry**[1]

INDUSTRIAL AND
COMMERCIAL COMPANIES [2]

MANUFACTURING COMPANIES

1965  66  67  68  69  70  71  72  73  74  75  76  77  78  79  80  81

1. Gross operating surplus on UK operations (i.e. before tax and interest payments) less capital consumption, at current replacement cost.

2. Excluding North Sea exploration and productive activities.

*Source: British business,* 17th September 1982.

The growth of government consumption and non-manufacturing private fixed investment and, more recently, the strong rise in private consumption, were sufficient to generate a weak recovery in final domestic demand from mid-1981 (Table 1). The slowdown in destocking from the second half of 1981 onwards imparted a positive contribution to the growth of total domestic demand in 1982. Real GDP after falling sharply in 1980 and 1981, recovered somewhat – at a rate of 1½ per cent – in the first half of 1982, helped by a small positive contribution from the change in the real foreign balance also. Despite the unfavourable trends in the volume of exports and imports in the second half-year (see section on international trade and payments below), real GDP continued to grow moderately giving an overall growth rate of ¾ per cent in 1982 as a whole. Manufacturing output – reflecting the effects of the earlier marked loss of competitiveness and the weakness of world trade – was broadly unchanged in 1982 on a yearly basis but falling through the year.

*Labour market conditions*

The current recession has been characterised by a very sharp fall in total employment which has continued in 1982 although at a less rapid rate (Table 2). Between mid-1979 and late 1982, total employment is expected to have declined by

11

# Table 2. Labour market statistics

| | 1975 / 1963 Average | 1976 | 1977 | 1978 | 1979 | 1980 | 1981 | 1982 Q1 | 1982 Q2 | 1982 Q3 |
|---|---|---|---|---|---|---|---|---|---|---|
| | | Annual percentage rate of change | | | | | | Change over six months at annual rate | | |
| **Labour force s.a.[1]** | | | | | | | | | | |
| Labour force[2] | 0.2 | 0.9 | 0.7 | 0.6 | 0.6 | 0.9 | -0.1 | -1.1 | -1.0 | -0.7 |
| Employment, total | 0.1 | -0.5 | 0.2 | 0.8 | 0.9 | -1.7 | -3.8 | -2.1 | -2.0 | |
| Employees, total | 0.1 | -0.6 | 0.3 | 1.0 | 1.1 | -1.9 | -4.5 | -2.8 | -2.7 | |
| Males (percentage share) | (62.5) | (59.4) | (59.1) | (58.7) | (58.2) | (57.9) | (57.3) | (57.0) | (56.8) | |
| Females (percentage share) | (37.5) | (40.6) | (40.9) | (41.3) | (41.8) | (42.1) | (42.7) | (43.0) | (43.2) | |
| Production industries | -0.5 | -2.5 | -0.3 | -0.4 | -0.6 | -4.7 | -9.2 | -6.0 | -5.6 | -5.4 |
| of which: Manufacturing | -0.5 | -3.1 | 0.2 | -0.4 | -1.1 | -5.7 | -2.8 | -5.1 | -5.3 | -5.9 |
| Public administration[3] | 1.3 | -1.2 | -1.4 | -0.4 | -0.0 | -1.2 | -1.3 | -2.8 | -0.7 | |
| Other tertiary sectors[3] | 2.7 | 0.9 | 1.0 | 2.2 | 9.7 | -0.6 | -0.9 | -3.1 | -1.3 | |
| General government | 2.7 | 2.2 | -0.7 | 0.3 | 1.4 | -0.5 | -0.4 | | | |
| **Productivity[1][4]** | | | | | | | | | | |
| Total economy | 2.3 | 2.0 | 1.3 | 1.7 | 0.0 | -1.3 | 1.6 | 2.3 | 2.0 | |
| Manufacturing | 2.7 | 5.3 | 1.6 | 1.1 | 1.3 | -3.7 | 3.9 | 4.7 | 3.8 | 3.5 |
| **Unemployment s.a.[5]** | | | | | | | | | | |
| Total (excluding school leavers) | | | | | | | | | | |
| U.K.: Thousands | 565 | 1 273 | 1 378 | 1 376 | 1 307 | 1 668 | 2 539 | 2 817 | 2 877 | 2 984 |
| Rate[6] | 2.4 | 5.3 | 5.7 | 5.7 | 5.4 | 6.8 | 10.6 | 11.8 | 12.0 | 12.5 |
| Total (excluding school leavers) | | | | | | | | | | |
| G.B.: Thousands | 529 | 1 223 | 1 323 | 1 316 | 1 248 | 1 596 | 2 442 | 2 713 | 2 769 | 2 872 |
| Rate[6] | 2.3 | 5.2 | 5.6 | 5.6 | 5.2 | 6.7 | 10.5 | 11.6 | 11.9 | 12.3 |
| Males: Thousands | 436 | 941 | 976 | 947 | 879 | 1 117 | 1 768 | 1 965 | 2 001 | 2 073 |
| Rate[6] | 3.0 | 6.7 | 6.9 | 6.7 | 6.3 | 7.9 | 12.8 | 14.2 | 14.4 | 15.0 |
| Females: Thousands | 93 | 282 | 347 | 369 | 369 | 479 | 675 | 748 | 768 | 799 |
| Rate[6] | 1.1 | 3.0 | 3.7 | 3.9 | 3.8 | 4.9 | 7.1 | 7.9 | 8.1 | 8.5 |
| Structure of unemployment, n.s.a. | | | | | | | | | | |
| By duration (percentage share) | | | | | | | | | | |
| Up to 4 weeks | .. | (19.5) | (18.5) | (17.6) | (17.3) | (17.7) | (12.0) | (8.6) | (8.9) | (12.2) |
| More than 4 weeks | .. | (80.5) | (81.5) | (82.4) | (82.7) | (82.3) | (88.0) | (91.4) | (91.1) | (87.8) |
| By age (percentage share) | | | | | | | | | | |
| Under 18 | .. | (14.1) | (14.5) | (14.2) | (9.7) | (11.5) | (9.3) | (7.5) | (6.4) | (11.6) |
| 18 to 24 | .. | (26.2) | (26.6) | (26.7) | (27.7) | (28.6) | (30.0) | (30.1) | (30.3) | (29.0) |
| 25 to 59 | .. | (49.7) | (49.7) | (50.0) | (52.8) | (51.3) | (53.0) | (54.9) | (55.8) | (52.3) |
| 60 and over | .. | (10.0) | (9.2) | (9.1) | (9.8) | (8.6) | (7.7) | (7.5) | (7.5) | (7.1) |
| **Memorandum items:** | | | | | | | | | | |
| Unemployment ratio, U.K.[7] | 2.3 | 5.2 | 5.6 | 5.5 | 5.2 | 6.9 | 10.4 | 11.2 | 11.6 | 12.1 |
| Average hours worked per operative G.B.: Manufacturing (1975=100) | 104.9 | 100.3 | 101.3 | 101.1 | 100.9 | 98.2 | 97.0 | 97.6 | 98.2 | 98.6 |
| Vacancies U.K., thousands | 211.1 | 119.7 | 155.9 | 210.3 | 241.3 | 143.0 | 97.0 | 111.7 | 107.2 | 110.9 |

1. United Kingdom.
2. OECD Secretariat estimates based on the more recent data of the 1981 Census of Employment.
3. Great Britain.
4. Productivity is based on the output-measure of GDP excluding North Sea oil.
5. Unemployment is based on the old definition which includes job seekers not entitled to receive unemployment benefits.
6. As a per cent of employees (employed and unemployed). This is the official U.K. measure.
7. As a per cent of total labour force, including school leavers.
*Source: Department of Employment Gazette.*

about 9 per cent, more than can be explained by cyclical factors. In the previous recession (following the first oil crisis), total dependent employment[6] was largely unchanged, falling by just over 1 per cent in the two years to 1976. In the next three years, dependent employment rose relatively rapidly to reach by mid-1979 its highest level since 1967. In view of the weak recovery of output (real non-oil GDP in 1979 was only 3¼ per cent above the previous peak in 1973), the rapid growth of employment in

6. Total employees in employment.

12

the three years to 1979 is surprising. It seems that business sentiment may not have adjusted to the fundamental change in economic conditions after the first oil shock and that companies were prepared to hire labour in the expectation that the strength of the recovery would not differ greatly from earlier recoveries.

From the onset of the second oil crisis, businessmen realised that a difficult period of adjustment was necessary before the economy could get back on a sustained growth path, which in any case would be considerably weaker over the medium term compared with past trends. Also, reflecting mainly the deterioration in external competitiveness, economic conditions worsened significantly faster than in earlier recessions. This was reflected in a marked increase in labour costs in relation to the rise in the value of output; despite considerable labour shedding, total labour costs increased from about 69½ per cent of GDP[7] in the three years to 1978 to 72¾ per cent in 1979 and 76¾ per cent in 1981, some 4½ percentage points higher than the previous high point in 1975. The financial pressure on companies caused them to start reducing their workforce before the fall in output became apparent. This behaviour was markedly different to that in earlier recessions in which the decline in employment lagged output by some three quarters on average. Changing trade union attitudes, given that many companies risked bankruptcy unless labour saving economies were made, may help explain the rapidity with which workforces were reduced without major industrial disruption.

The decline in dependent employment was widespread but it was particularly marked in industry which experienced an annual rate of decline of 8 per cent in the two years to end-1981 (Diagram 3). The comparable figure for services was 1¼ per cent. The decline in dependent employment slowed down during the first nine months of 1982 to about 2½ per cent annual rate, but employment in industry continued to fall at a rate about four times that for services (5¼ per cent and 1¼ per cent respectively). This differential pattern reflects:

Diagram 3. **Sectoral employment trends**

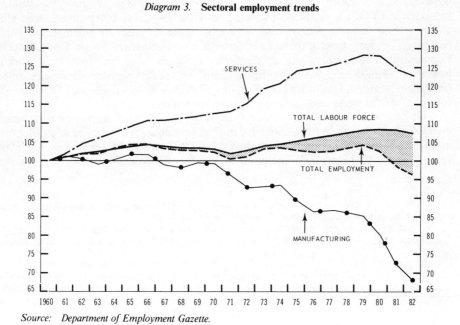

Source: *Department of Employment Gazette.*

7. Total compensation of employees (including National Insurance Surcharge) divided by GDP at factor cost, excluding North Sea oil and gas output.

13

*i)*  The much larger fall in manufacturing than services output; between 1979 and early 1982 the respective falls were 15 and 1½ per cent.

*ii)*  Labour costs rose more in manufacturing than in services; in manufacturing they rose from about 73¾ per cent of value added in the two years to 1978 to about 82½ per cent in 1981.

*iii)*  Labour hoarding in manufacturing up to 1980 – as indicated by the sharper deceleration in the rate of growth of productivity in manufacturing after the mid-1970s[8] – was more important than in services.

To some extent, the decline in employment since 1979 reflects a reversal of labour hoarding in the previous four years. The substantial labour shedding raised the growth of productivity (output per man) in manufacturing to 4 per cent in 1981 and to some 5¾ per cent in 1982. Allowing for a decline in hours worked, productivity growth per man-hour was even stronger. Despite this improvement, however, the annual growth of productivity in manufacturing between the mid-1970s and 1982 of about 2 per cent was still lower than the trend rate in the past. Reflecting falling employment, productivity growth in services has also accelerated since 1979 to an estimated 1¾ per cent in 1982 compared with an average rate of a little over ½ per cent during the previous six years.

The effects of falling employment on registered unemployment were mitigated by a decline in the labour force, reflecting the "discouraged worker" effect and voluntary early retirements. Accordingly, after an uninterrupted increase of about ¾ per cent per annum in the eight years to 1980, the total labour force has fallen since 1980 (Table 2), with the decline reaching about ¾ per cent annual rate in 1982[9]. Similarly, the authorities expanded the employment-creating and training schemes which were first introduced in the second half of the 1970s. These schemes covered some 560 000 persons in mid-1982 (at a cost of £1½ billion in 1982/83) compared with 300 000 in 1979. The net effect of these schemes on the unemployment register is somewhat smaller, however, and is estimated at about 300 000 in 1982. The Youth Opportunities Programme (YOP) is the largest scheme, covering some 210 000 people in mid-1982 and providing training courses and work experience schemes for unemployed young persons. The next most important scheme is the Temporary Short Time Working Compensation Scheme, which encourages employers to adopt short time working instead of redundancies, with subsidies paid at the rate of 50 per cent of normal earnings (including National Insurance contributions). The Job Release Scheme (JRS) has also considerable coverage and encourages early retirement.[10]

Despite the fall in the labour force and the various employment schemes, unemployment has risen from about 1.4 million (including unemployed school-leavers) in 1979 to some 3¼ million towards the end of 1982, or from 5 per cent of the labour force to nearly 12½ per cent[11]. Including involuntary drop-outs from the labour market,

---

8.  Productivity growth in manufacturing in the six years to 1980 was an average annual rate of around ½ per cent, about four-fifths lower than the longer-run rate up to 1973/74.

9.  Labour force figures are OECD estimates based on the more recent data of the 1981 Census of Employment which shows that total employment was about 700 000 more in mid-1982 than previously estimated.

10.  See Annex II for a fuller analysis of the employment and training schemes.

11.  The United Kingdom authorities changed the definitions of unemployment in November 1982. Under the previous system – used in this Survey – unemployed were considered those registered for work in Job Centres, irrespective of whether or not they claimed unemployment benefit. Under the new system, only those claiming unemployment benefits will be registered as unemployed in the Benefit Offices, i.e. this excludes many married women not entitled to benefits and a few other categories. The other main differences are: under the new system severely disabled unemployed people are now for the first time included (estimated at about 23 000); in the Benefit Offices the count is based on computer (rather than the man count in the Job

*(Continued on next page)*

actual unemployment is somewhat higher. This, together with voluntary early retirement, helps explain the fall in the proportion of unemployed in the "60 and over" group since 1979 (Table 2). The rise of female unemployment was somewhat slower than that of males. Despite the employment schemes which favour young people, persons under 24 years – accounting for about 40 per cent of total registered unemployed – continued to suffer more than other age-groups. The steep rise in unemployment was accompanied by a marked increase in the duration of unemployment; the share of those unemployed for more than one year was 33½ per cent of the total in mid-1982 compared with just less than 20 per cent two years earlier while the share of those unemployed for between six months and one year rose from 16 per cent to 21½ per cent.

## Costs and prices

After falling substantially in 1981, the rate of inflation declined further in 1982 (Diagram 4) and to a greater extent than generally expected. The year-on-year increase in retail prices fell from 12 per cent in 1981 to nearly 5½ per cent in December 1982 with most components contributing to the slowdown. The sharp deceleration in retail price rises since mid-1982 reflects mainly sizeable reductions in mortgage rates and

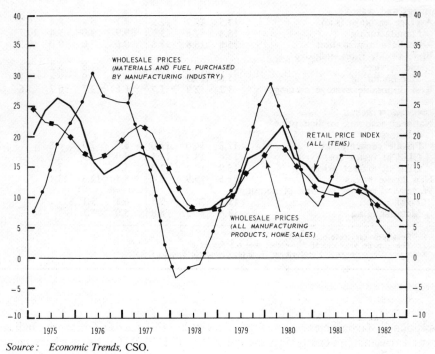

*Diagram 4.* **Price trends**
Percentage rate of change from previous year

*Source : Economic Trends,* CSO.

*(Note 11 continued)*
Centres) and therefore is more up to date, lowering registered unemployed by 100 000 in November 1982 and 78 000 on average in the first ten months of 1982. In October 1982 the number of registered unemployed under the new system was 3 049 000 and under the old system 3 295 100, i.e. 246 100 less under the new system (the same average difference was recorded in the first ten months of 1982).

15

Table 3.  Costs and prices
Percentage change at annual rate

| | 1979 | 1980 | 1981 | Q1 | Q2 | 1982 Q3 | Oct. | Nov. |
|---|---|---|---|---|---|---|---|---|
| | Annual average | | | Change over six months earlier | | | | |
| Retail prices, total | 13.4 | 18.0 | 11.9 | 8.5 | 10.1 | 7.5 | 3.0 | 2.6[2] |
| Total, excluding seasonal food | 13.3 | 18.4 | 11.9 | 7.5 | 9.0 | 8.5 | 4.7 | 4.5 |
| Food | 12.0 | 12.1 | 8.4 | 14.0 | 13.4 | −0.5 | −4.0 | −4.4 |
| Non-food | 13.8 | 19.7 | 12.8 | 7.1 | 9.3 | 9.6 | 4.8 | 4.4 |
| of which: | | | | | | | | |
| Housing | 20.5 | 29.0 | 18.1 | 14.5 | 12.8 | 10.6 | −2.5 | −1.8 |
| Fuel and light | 10.1 | 25.0 | 21.3 | 7.5 | 14.7 | 19.5 | 16.4 | 15.6 |
| Services | 11.4 | 22.8 | 14.5 | 17.8 | 11.3 | 4.0 | 2.2 | 3.1 |
| Durables | 10.9 | 12.1 | 4.8 | 2.2 | 2.6 | 2.3 | 1.6 | 2.4 |
| Clothing and footwear | 9.5 | 9.7 | 1.4 | 0.4 | 0.0 | 1.8 | 1.9 | 2.5 |
| Nationalised industries | 8.5 | 24.8 | 19.5 | 7.5 | 21.0 | 20.1 | 8.9 | 9.0 |
| Wholesale prices, total | | | | | | | | |
| Materials and fuel purchased by manufacturing industry | 15.9 | 19.9 | 13.6 | 2.0 | 2.3 | 5.7 | 6.1 | 12.0 |
| All manufacturing products, home sales | 12.2 | 16.3 | 10.7 | 9.3 | 8.0 | 6.7 | 6.6 | 6.9 |
| Import prices (average values) | 8.1 | 10.5 | 3.8 | 7.0 | −1.6 | 0.4 | 4.5 | 3.5 |
| Crude oil | 18.3 | 56.0 | 31.0 | 14.1 | −7.8 | 3.0 | 31.3 | 22.3 |
| Non-oil goods | 6.3 | 6.9 | 2.3 | 6.0 | 2.8 | 2.3 | 1.3 | −0.5 |
| Earnings and wages | | | | | | | | |
| Average earnings (s.a.) | 15.5 | 20.7 | 12.9 | 8.7 | 6.4 | 8.4 | 8.5 | |
| Manufacturing | 15.6 | 17.8 | 13.2 | 9.9 | 9.0 | 9.4 | 10.7 | |
| Public administration | 16.8 | 26.6 | 13.6 | 0.6 | 7.0 | 9.0 | 10.5 | |
| Basic weekly rates, industry and services | 15.0 | 18.0 | 10.2 | 6.9 | 7.8 | 5.2 | 2.9 | 2.1 |
| Manufacturing | 15.0 | 17.1 | 9.4 | 7.8 | 5.9 | 2.8 | 2.1 | 1.1 |
| Real disposable average earnings[1] | 3.2 | 2.9 | −1.7 | −1.1 | −2.7 | 0.7 | 3.6 | 6.0 |
| Memorandum items: | | | | | | | | |
| National accounts implicit price deflators | | | | | | | | |
| Private consumption | 12.8 | 16.0 | 11.0 | 8.0 | 7.7 | 6.8 | | |
| GDP at factor cost | 13.4 | 18.4 | 11.1 | 4.0 | 7.5 | 8.1 | | |
| GDP at market prices | 15.0 | 19.2 | 12.2 | 5.2 | 8.8 | 7.2 | | |
| New house prices | 28.5 | 19.9 | 2.4 | −6.1 | −12.3 | 11.1 | | |
| Wages and salaries per unit of output | | | | | | | | |
| Total | 15.2 | 20.3 | 9.5 | 6.3 | 5.1 | | | |
| Manufacturing | 13.8 | 22.2 | 8.8 | 5.0 | 5.1 | | | |

1. Real (post-tax) take-home pay.
2. The year on year rate to November was 6.3 per cent.
*Sources: Department of Employment Gazette; Economic Trends, CSO.*

exceptionally favourable seasonal food prices in the third quarter. Other price indicators have also eased significantly since the end of 1981 (Table 3). The rise in wholesale prices slowed down appreciably, particularly input prices which have benefited from the weakness of import prices. Largely influenced by this favourable trend, the annual rate of increase of wholesale prices of manufactured products (home sales) decelerated sharply to some 7 per cent during the first eleven months of 1982. Due to severe world competition associated with the loss of competitiveness in previous years and reflecting companies' efforts not to exacerbate the trend loss in export market shares, the increase in the price of manufactured exports continued to be fairly slow (4½ per cent annual rate) during the first eleven months of 1982, considerably slower than that of home sales. The only exception to this downward trend during 1982 was the increase in the price of new dwellings, but in September their price was still below the peak in the spring of 1981.

The growth of unit labour costs has fallen markedly from 20 per cent (annual rate) during the eighteen months to the end of 1980 to 7½ per cent during 1981 followed by a further small deceleration to an estimated 4 per cent (annual rate) during 1982. The latter is the slowest rise since 1970. The steep decline over the last two years reflected both the upturn in productivity and more importantly the slowdown in the growth of average earnings. The direct contribution of unit labour costs to the rise in the consumer price deflator (national accounts implicit private consumption deflator) fell from 10½ percentage points in 1980 to just less than 3½ percentage points on average in the two half years of 1982 (Table 4). Though profits (excluding North Sea oil activities) recovered somewhat from the exceptionally low level in 1981, they remained depressed thus exerting downward pressure on prices, as highlighted by the overall weak contribution of profits and other domestic costs to the rise in the consumer price deflator (Table 4). The sluggishness in activity during the second half of 1982 may have affected the recovery in profits.

Table 4. **Contributions to price increases**

Percentage point contributions to the annual rate of increase of consumer deflator

| | Annual rate of change from previous period | | | | | | | |
|---|---|---|---|---|---|---|---|---|
| | 1978 | 1979 | 1980 | 1981 | 1982 | 1981 II | 1982 I | 1982 II¹ |
| Unit labour costs | 5¼ | 7½ | 10½ | 6¾ | 4 | 6¼ | 4 | 3 |
| Profits and other domestic sectors | ¾ | 1¼ | ¼ | ¼ | ½ | ¼ | ¾ | ½ |
| Import prices² | 1½ | 1¾ | 2½ | 1¾ | 1½ | 2¼ | 1½ | 1¼ |
| Net indirect taxes | 1 | 3 | 2¾ | 2¼ | 1½ | 1¾ | 1 | 1 |
| Total above | 8½ | 13½ | 16 | 11 | 7½ | 10¾ | 7½ | 6 |
| Residual³ | ¼ | −¾ | ¼ | — | ½ | — | ½ | — |
| Consumer price deflator | 8¾ | 12¾ | 16¼ | 11 | 8 | 10¾ | 8 | 6 |

1. Secretariat estimates. Unit labour costs are based on the underlying rate of increase of average earnings.
2. Implicit deflator of imports of goods.
3. The residual reflects principally changes in weights and in lag structures, and certain seasonal elements.
*Sources: National Income and Expenditure* 1982 edition; *Economic Trends,* CSO; the current account of the United Kingdom Balance of Payments, Department of Trade and OECD Secretariat estimates.

Import prices also exerted downward pressure on the consumer price deflator; after rising by some 12 per cent during 1981 they remained flat during 1982. An important factor behind this favourable trend is the weakness in world commodity and oil prices. World recession has also helped to stem the rise in manufactured goods prices in world markets and resulted in a sharp deceleration in the rate of growth of import prices of manufactures to 2¼ per cent annual rate during the first ten months of 1982. Accordingly, after allowing for lags in coming through to final prices, the direct contribution of import prices to the rise in the consumer price deflator is estimated to have slowed to about 1¼ percentage points in the second half of 1982. In addition to the direct effects, low import prices generally put appreciable downward pressure on prices of domestic manufactures as companies attempted to curb import penetration and hold onto their share of home markets. The contribution of import prices to the slowdown in the rate of inflation is therefore probably considerably stronger than suggested by the direct effects only[12] (Table 4).

After the sharp deceleration during 1981 to some 10 per cent, the year-on-year increase in average earnings remained broadly stable during the first half of 1982 before falling to 8¾ per cent (underlying rate) in October (Table 3). As in the previous year, the increase in earnings in industry in 1982 was higher than in the other sectors, partly because of a small increase in hours worked from the low level in 1981 and also because many wage settlements in industry included productivity clauses.[13] In addition to the normal wagedrift, the above factors explain the large difference in the year-on-year rise between basic weekly wage rates and average earnings over the last couple of years (Table 3). The increase in earnings in services was about 3 percentage points less than in industry, reflecting some delays in settling pay increases in parts of the public sector, and also the Government's determination to curb the growth of earnings in the public sector which, though somewhat higher than had been officially provided for, still remained fairly low in relation to pay increases in other sectors.

## International trade and payments

Recent developments in the balance of payments are summarised in Table 5. The exceptionally high current external surplus in 1981 reflected weak non-oil imports as stocks were run down, a substantial improvement in the non-oil terms of trade and a large invisible surplus. There was a marked weakening in the first eleven months of 1982 in the trade and invisible accounts and especially in the non-oil trade account. This was mainly due to volume changes. The rising trend in food exports in volume in the ten years to 1981 was reversed. The weakening of non-oil merchandise exports was offset by rising oil exports leading to broadly stable total merchandise exports (volume) in 1982 as a whole. The volume of manufactured imports – notably cars and intermediate and capital goods – increased strongly in 1981 and the upward trend has continued in 1982. Oil and basic material imports have been falling in 1982 but the volume of total merchandise imports is expected to be about 5½ per cent higher than in 1981. Reflecting largely these volume developments, the trade surplus in 1982 has fallen sharply from the high 1981 level. Excluding oil, however, the trade account is in substantial and increasing deficit; in the first eleven months of 1982 the non-oil trade deficit was running at an annual rate of $4½ billion compared with an annual average deficit of $1 billion during the 1970s.[14]

After continuous growth during the 1970s there has been remarkable stability in the services' surplus between end-1978 and mid-1982. However, this overall development masks important differences in the behaviour of various components; in particular, the travel account – reflecting partly the loss of competitiveness – turned around from a large surplus up to 1979 to a small deficit since 1981 and the sea transport account also showed a small deficit in 1981 and in the first nine months of 1982. In contrast, given the significant comparative advantage enjoyed by the United Kingdom and the expansion of international borrowing, the financial services' surplus has risen appreciably since 1980. The interest and profits and dividend account has continued to experience large fluctuations in recent years. Despite the increase in earnings due to the surge in portfolio investment abroad (after the abolition of foreign exchange controls in 1979), the surplus

12.   This effect is partly captured by the low contribution of profits to the rise in the consumer price deflator.

13.   These clauses were proposed by companies with the aim both to stimulate productivity growth and also to make acceptable to unions the small increase in basic wage rates and cuts in labour force.

14.   The only year in the post-war period in which the non-oil deficit was larger was 1979.

18

Diagram 5. **External Trade**

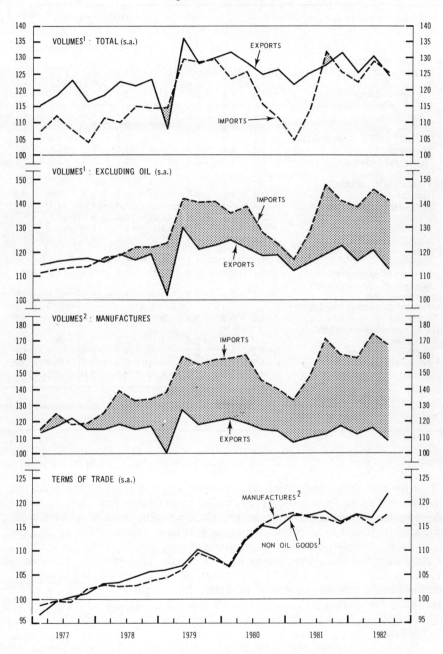

1. Balance of payments basis.
2. Customs basis.
*Sources: Monthly review of External Trade Statistics* and OECD Secretariat estimates.

19

Table 5. **Balance of payments**
$ billion, annual rate

| | 1978 | 1979 | 1980 | 1981 | 1981 I | 1981 II | 1982 I | 1982 Q3 | 1982 Oct.-Nov. average |
|---|---|---|---|---|---|---|---|---|---|
| **Seasonally adjusted** | | | | | | | | | |
| Exports, fob | 67.3 | 86.2 | 110.2 | 102.7 | 104.8 | 100.5 | 97.9 | 94.3 | 96.2 |
| Imports, fob | 70.2 | 93.5 | 107.4 | 96.6 | 93.0 | 100.2 | 96.3 | 91.5 | 89.0 |
| Trade balance | −3.0 | −7.3 | 2.8 | 6.1 | 11.8 | 0.3 | 1.6 | 2.8 | 7.2 |
| of which: Non-oil | 0.8 | −5.8 | 2.1 | 0.3 | 5.1 | −4.4 | −4.2 | −5.9 | −2.8 |
| Invisibles, net | 4.9 | 5.5 | 3.9 | 6.1 | 6.7 | 5.4 | 4.3 | 4.1 | 3.5 |
| Services, net | 7.1 | 8.4 | 9.4 | 8.0 | 8.9 | 7.1 | 7.6 | 6.7 | |
| Interest, profits and dividends | 1.2 | 1.9 | −0.6 | 2.0 | 2.5 | 1.5 | 0.8 | 1.1 | |
| Transfers | −3.4 | −4.8 | −4.9 | −3.9 | −4.7 | −3.2 | −4.1 | −3.7 | |
| Current balance | 2.0 | −1.8 | 6.7 | 12.1 | 18.5 | 5.8 | 5.9 | 6.9 | 10.7 |
| **Not seasonally adjusted** | | | | | | | | | |
| Current balance | 2.0 | −1.8 | 6.7 | 12.1 | 16.8 | 7.5 | 4.4 | 8.2 | |
| Long-term capital, net | −7.3 | −6.2 | −11.5 | −17.2 | −23.0 | −11.3 | −14.4 | | |
| Private | −7.1 | −5.3 | −9.8 | −14.0 | −18.1 | −9.9 | −13.6 | | |
| Official | −0.3 | −0.8 | −1.6 | −3.1 | −4.9 | −1.4 | −0.8 | −13.0 | |
| Basic balance | −5.4 | −8.0 | −4.8 | −5.0 | −6.3 | −3.8 | −10.0 | | |
| Non-monetary short-term capital | 0.2 | −0.5 | −1.3 | 0.1 | 1.5 | −1.2 | −0.2 | | |
| Errors and omissions | 4.1 | 0.7 | −1.0 | −2.3 | 5.8 | −10.5 | −7.1 | −4.2 | |
| Balance of non-monetary transactions | −1.1 | −7.8 | −7.2 | −7.2 | 1.1 | −15.5 | −17.3 | −9.0 | |
| Private monetary short-term capital | −1.2 | 9.3 | 4.8 | 2.1 | −7.3 | 11.5 | 14.2 | 6.0 | |
| Net transactions of monetary authorities | −2.3 | 1.5 | −2.4 | −5.1 | −6.2 | −4.0 | −3.0 | −3.0 | |
| Sterling liabilities | −0.2 | 1.6 | 2.9 | 0.2 | 1.1 | −0.6 | 0.9 | 1.2 | |
| Other financing[1] | −1.9 | −0.9 | 0.1 | — | 0.4 | −0.3 | −0.4 | −0.2 | |
| Changes in reserves | −4.5 | 2.2 | 0.7 | −4.9 | −4.8 | −5.0 | −2.5 | −2.0 | |

1. Including SDR allocations.
*Sources: Economic Trends*, CSO; The Current Account of the United Kingdom Balance of Payments, Press Notice, Department of Trade.

of the interest, profits and dividends' account contracted considerably in the first nine months of 1982, and with a small rise in net government transfers, there was a decline in the invisible surplus in the latter period. On the capital account, private investment overseas continued to be substantial in the first nine months of 1982, rising portfolio investment roughly offsetting falling direct investment. Overseas investment in the United Kingdom though remaining high, declined a little in the first nine months of 1982. In total, the deficit of the investment and other capital transactions' account declined in the first nine months of 1982, but this was partly offset by a large negative balancing item so that despite the current account surplus there were some drawings on official reserves, (partly to support sterling) whose level at the end of 1982 were about $17 billion.[15]

The recent deterioration of the non-oil trade account – largely because of trade in manufactures – represents a continuation of a long-term trend involving large losses of

15. Including the valuation effect due to the fall in the price of gold and the changes in parities of convertible currencies (which accounted for about $2¾ billion and $1¼ billion respectively) the fall in reserves was $6½ billion during 1982.

export market shares in the post-war period. Since the first oil crisis and until 1979, trade performance in manufactures did not deteriorate at the same average rate as in the 1960s and early 1970s. The slowdown in the loss of market shares reflected partly the end of the adjustment to special factors such as changing Commonwealth preferences and partly the substantial fall of sterling's effective exchange rate which resulted in considerable decline in relative unit labour costs between 1971/72 and 1977 (Diagram 6). Other contributing factors were, first, the commodity structure of manufactures which seems to have had a favourable, if small, effect on export growth[16] and secondly, membership of the EEC has been accompanied by gains in market shares in manufactures in the EEC. In all other markets – despite the favourable factors – considerable loss of shares was recorded (Table 6), total volume losses amounting to about 2½ per cent on average each year between 1974 and 1979.

Trade developments changed importantly following the unprecedented big deterioration in external competitiveness after 1977. The increase in relative unit labour costs was about 45 per cent between the average level of the five years to 1977 and 1982[17]. In the first few years following 1977, higher labour costs reflected in export prices considerably raised the value of manufactured exports resulting in substantial gains in market shares in value in the four years to 1980. However, as time passed, the effects on export volumes of high export prices and relative costs began to gather strength to give historically big losses in export market shares (volume) in manufactures. Indeed, the cumulative volume loss in export market shares in manufactures has amounted to 25 per cent in the last five years which is as much as during the previous ten years. With the volume losses outweighing the price rises, the United Kingdom reverted

Table 6.  **Regional distribution of manufactured exports[1]**

| | Average market growth | | Share of UK manufactures in world exports of manufactures | | Regional distribution of UK exports | | Average market gains (+) or losses (−) | |
|---|---|---|---|---|---|---|---|---|
| | 1972 / 1966 | 1980 / 1972 | 1966/ 1967 | 1979/ 1980 | 1966/ 1967 | 1979/ 1980 | 1972 / 1966 | 1980 / 1972 |
| OECD | 14.6 | 18.6 | 10.5 | 8.0 | 64.5 | 62.6 | −4.9 | −0.3 |
| *of which:* | | | | | | | | |
| United States | 18.6 | 15.9 | 10.0 | 6.8 | 11.0 | 8.2 | −5.9 | −2.0 |
| EEC | 15.8 | 20.5 | 8.0 | 8.1 | 23.6 | 36.3 | −4.2 | 3.0 |
| Other OECD[2] | 11.7 | 15.4 | 14.6 | 7.2 | 14.4 | 6.2 | −7.9 | −5.0 |
| Non-OECD | 11.3 | 24.2 | 13.4 | 7.2 | 35.5 | 37.4 | −3.6 | −3.0 |
| *of which:* | | | | | | | | |
| OPEC | 13.2 | 33.6 | 13.9 | 9.8 | 5.4 | 9.8 | −2.6 | −2.5 |
| COMECON | 17.7 | 20.4 | 11.5 | 6.3 | 3.7 | 2.5 | −6.9 | −3.5 |
| Other developing countries | 10.2 | 22.3 | 13.7 | 10.5 | 26.5 | 25.0 | −3.2 | −2.0 |
| Total | 14.1 | 21.0 | 11.4 | 8.1 | 100.0 | 100.0 | −4.5 | −1.1 |

1. In current prices.
2. Japan, Australia, Canada and New Zealand.
*Source:* OECD Secretariat.

16.   The relatively big share of textiles in British exports which was one of the least dynamic sectors in total OECD exports, was more than offset by the relatively large share of products with above average growth in world demand, such as, aircraft, electrical machinery, scientific instruments etc.

17.   The effective appreciation of sterling contributed about 5 percentage points to the 45 per cent rise in relative unit labour costs over this period and excessive pay rises coupled with low productivity contributed the additional 40 percentage points. The deterioration in terms of relative export prices of manufactures was 22 per cent between the average level in the five years to 1973 to 1977 and 1977 to 1982.

21

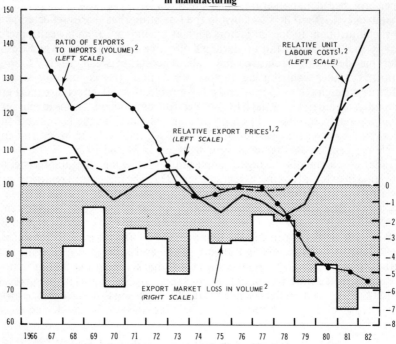

*Diagram 6.* **Price competitiveness and export performance in manufacturing**

RATIO OF EXPORTS TO IMPORTS (VOLUME)[2] *(LEFT SCALE)*

RELATIVE UNIT LABOUR COSTS[1,2] *(LEFT SCALE)*

RELATIVE EXPORT PRICES[1,2] *(LEFT SCALE)*

EXPORT MARKET LOSS IN VOLUME[2] *(RIGHT SCALE)*

1. Lagged one year.
2. Two year moving average.
*Source:* OECD Secretariat estimates.

since 1981 to its traditional pattern of small market losses in value as well. Moreover, the initial important export market gains in the EEC, following the United Kingdom's membership, began to fade towards the end of the 1970s. Because of the loss of price competitiveness, exports of consumer goods, notably passenger cars, suffered most, and continued to experience sizeable volume declines in 1982; the cumulative decline of passenger cars was about one-third since 1977/78 and for other consumer goods nearly 15 per cent. However, reflecting exporters' desire to hold onto market shares, export prices have risen slowly over the last two years which coupled with the effective depreciation of sterling in the second half of 1982 restored relative export prices of manufactures at the end of 1982 to the 1979 level (which was still one-fifth above the average in the period 1973/1977). The improvement in relative export prices after the peak in early 1981 has limited the loss of export market shares to some 3 per cent in 1982, or a third of that in 1981.

As well as the longer-run loss of export market shares in manufactures, there has been substantial penetration of the home market by imports of manufactures. Import penetration[18] increased rapidly – by about 7 percentage points to 23¼ per cent of the home market – between 1970 and 1974 reflecting buoyant domestic demand and the loss of competitiveness up to 1972. The improvement in external competitiveness after 1972 largely explains the slowdown in the pace of import penetration between 1975 and

18. Manufactured imports as a per cent of total home demand for manufactures (e.g. manufacturers' sales plus imports less exports).

22

1979; the share of imports in the domestic market rose by only 2½ percentage points to 25¾ per cent despite the improved access by EEC partners after 1973 and the relatively rapid growth in domestic demand after 1975[19]. In 1980 and early 1981, deeper recession in the United Kingdom relative to the OECD area and related heavy destocking which has a high import content, more than offset the initial effects of the deterioration in external competitiveness so that the contraction of home demand was accompanied by a similar fall in the volume of non-oil imports. But since mid-1981, non-oil imports have risen rapidly (Diagram 5). Within the total of non-oil imports, manufactures increased fastest; their penetration of the home market since 1979 increased markedly as illustrated by the 16 per cent fall in manufacturing output and the 10 per cent rise in the volume of imports of manufactures.

## II.  ECONOMIC POLICIES

The present Government in its first Budget in June 1979 formulated restrictive economic policies with the principal aim of combatting inflation. These policies were further elaborated in the Medium-Term Financial Strategy (MTFS) presented in the 1980/81 Budget, the emphasis being placed on a progressive reduction in the Public Sector Borrowing Requirement (PSBR) and in the growth of money supply over the medium term. In addition to the direct effects, the announcement of declining annual monetary and fiscal targets together with consistent policies were expected to bear down importantly on inflationary expectations. At the same time, the authorities announced that they would enhance the role of market forces by reducing state aid and intervention in the business sector, including privatisation of some publicly-owned companies. The authorities have broadly adhered to these objectives, emphasising the advantages of maintaining steady policies, notably in order not to undermine the credibility of the anti-inflationary priority. Inflation and the PSBR have been reduced somewhat faster than had been expected but developments in other areas have not been as favourable as the authorities had hoped. The output and employment costs of bringing down inflation have been considerably greater than envisaged and partly because of this the desired supply adjustments failed to materialise in important fields. While weak external demand has compounded the problems of implementing policies, the market responses to the different measures and the adjustment mechanisms have often diverged from the authorities' expectations.

Exchange rate movements, which are neither easily predictable nor subject to the same policy leverages as domestic variables, have importantly influenced economic developments in recent years. Higher oil prices and the increased production of North Sea oil contributed considerably to the appreciation of sterling in 1979/80 but the appreciation was stronger than economic fundamentals or interest rate differentials could justify. Non-economic factors also help explain the continuing upward pressure on sterling, which coincided with a sharp rise in unit labour costs. This deterioration of external competitiveness has been a major reason for the disappointing developments in the real economy. In particular, the negative contribution of the non-oil real foreign balance lowered real GDP by about 1½ per cent on average in 1981 and 1982. The authorities have generally refrained from intervening in an important way in foreign exchange markets (except for smoothing operations). Until recently, high interest rates

19.  The annual rate of growth of total domestic demand between 1975 and 1979 was 3¼ per cent.

have supported a strong sterling rate, in line with the authorities' anti-inflationary objectives. In the 1981/82 and 1982/83 Budget Reports attention was placed on the exchange rate as a monetary indicator for assessing domestic monetary conditions.

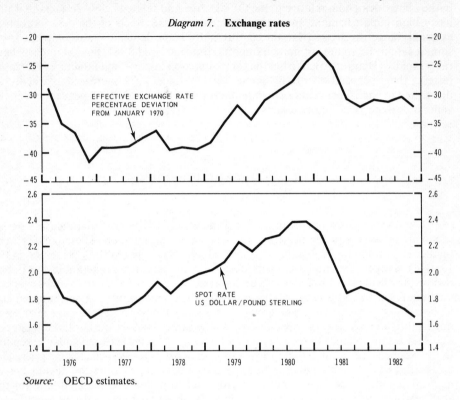

Diagram 7. **Exchange rates**

EFFECTIVE EXCHANGE RATE
PERCENTAGE DEVIATION
FROM JANUARY 1970

SPOT RATE
US DOLLAR / POUND STERLING

*Source:* OECD estimates.

## Fiscal policy

An unusually large fiscal swing was recorded between 1980/81 and 1981/82[20]. After rising by nearly one half in 1980/81, the General Government financial deficit[21] (GGFD) fell by rather more in 1981/82 to the equivalent of 1¾ per cent of GDP. The Budget projection was a GGFD of 2 per cent of GDP. The PSBR in 1981/82 was also below the planned level, falling by 2¼ percentage points to 3½ per cent of GDP. The stronger decline than originally estimated occurred despite somewhat weaker output growth and a higher increase in average pay in the public sector than projected and delays in tax receipts due to the Civil Service dispute in 1981/82[22]. Measuring fiscal changes and their impact on activity poses many problems. There is no unique way of

20. The financial year is from 1st April to 31st March. There has been a significant difference in GGFD and PSBR between calendar and financial years since 1980 largely due to the Civil Service dispute and the big delays in tax payments. These distortions have affected importantly the size of the fiscal impacts according to whether these are based on calendar or on financial years.
21. The GGFD is the United Kingdom term of "net lending" on a SNA basis, i.e. it excludes financial transactions.
22. The Central Government Borrowing Requirement (CGBR) in 1981/82 would have been up to £1¼ billion lower had there not been delays in tax collecting and additional interest payments due to the Civil Service dispute. This suggests that without the Civil Service dispute, the restrictive fiscal impact in 1981/82 would have been even stronger.

measurement and many of the longer-run effects on other parts of the economy have not yet been fully tested. In measuring the impact of fiscal action, the OECD emphasises the direct first-round effects and distinguishes between active (ex ante) actions and passive responses in the cycle. Allowing for the impact of automatic stabilisers (due to the decline in real GDP of 1¼ per cent between 1980/81 and 1981/82) the cyclically adjusted budget tightening (produced by the lower real GGFD) is estimated at about 3½ per cent of GDP, the largest in the OECD area and significantly more than had been budgeted for[23]. The restrictive budgetary impact was particularly strong in the last six months of the financial year when there were accelerated tax payments due to the delays earlier in the year. The smaller deficits reflected to a great extent increased discipline of central government departments under cash limits[24] and local authorities who in order to limit rate (local taxes) increases, restricted expenditure. Moreover, it seems that whenever overruns occurred on certain items there were more than compensating cuts on other items. These reductions were mainly concentrated on investment, illustrated by the substantial shortfall in government and public corporation's investment[25]. Similarly, lending to the private sector was severely curtailed[26].

The main projections of the 1982/83 Budget are summarised in Table 7[27]. The discretionary expenditure changes suggest a small tightening of the fiscal stance reflecting mainly the projected increase in government wages and salaries at a slower rate than inflation. However, the revenue measures provided for a small stimulus largely through an increase in income tax allowances and thresholds and some social security benefits. Also, some indirect taxes – notably excise duties – were increased less than indicated by full indexation to prices. The loss in revenue from the one percentage point reduction of the National Insurance Surcharge paid by employers will be partly offset by the corresponding increase in employee's national insurance contributions[28], which are required to balance the National Insurance Fund. The Budget and subsequent proposals also included some measures to improve the supply side of the economy (tax relief for companies, extension of employment schemes, energy price concessions) which are estimated to have a revenue cost of about £200 million in 1982/83 and about £600 million in a full year. As more than one-third of the latter represents tax relief on North Sea oil companies, the demand effect will be relatively small.

The outcome in 1982/83 will probably differ somewhat from the Budget projections. First, when the 1982/83 Budget was presented, the shortfalls in the GGFD and the PSBR in 1981/82 were unknown; secondly, it appears that part of the shortfall will continue (despite additional £¾ billion for the "Falkland Islands Task Force"), suggesting a continuing tighter fiscal policy posture than had been assumed in the MTFS and, thirdly, both inflation and real growth in 1982/83 are now expected to be lower than had been forecast in the Budget. During the first half of 1982/83 the PSBR

---

23. Due to the important structural and behavioural changes over the last few years, the fiscal impact does not pretend to be a precise figure but gives only the order of magnitude. In addition, the distortions arising from the Civil Service dispute and changing seasonal factors have also affected the figures since 1981. The impact from ex-ante budget changes because of the multiplier effects is usually spread over a number of years and denotes the thrust of policy.

24. About two-fifths of total central government expenditure is "cash limited", i.e. overruns are penalised and have to be corrected.

25. Despite a higher rate of inflation than expected, government investment declined (in value) by 24 per cent compared with a Budget forecast of 10 per cent, whereas investment by public corporations increased in value by 3½ per cent instead of 20 per cent in the Budget.

26. It is not clear whether certain funds which were budgeted to be lent directly from the public to the private sector were finally provided by commercial banks with the Government's approval.

27. For details of the Budget measures see Calendar of Main Economic Events.

28. The reduction in the National Insurance Surcharge was announced in the Budget, and the higher national insurance contributions in December 1981.

Table 7.  **Budgetary developments**

| | 1977/78 | 1978/79 | 1979/80 | 1980/81 | 1981/82 | Budget 1982/83 | |
|---|---|---|---|---|---|---|---|
| | | | | | | 1981/82 | 1982/83 |
| | | | Actual outturns | | | Esti-mated outturn | Forecast |
| Current receipts, total | 57.6 | 64.4 | 80.2 | 94.8 | 111.2 | 109.9 | 119.6 |
| of which: | | | | | | | |
| Taxes on income | 20.7 | 23.0 | 26.9 | 31.8 | 38.0 | 37.9 | 39.9 |
| Taxes on expenditure | 20.8 | 24.0 | 32.7 | 38.1 | 44.9 | 45.4 | 49.5 |
| National insurance contributions | 9.8 | 10.2 | 12.0 | 14.4 | 16.6 | 17.0 | 19.6 |
| Interest, dividends, etc. | 2.8 | 3.0 | 3.4 | 4.0 | 4.6 | 4.1 | 4.9 |
| | | | | | | | |
| Current expenditure, total | 57.1 | 65.6 | 79.1 | 96.4 | 110.4 | 109.4 | 117.9 |
| Final consumption | 30.2 | 33.9 | 40.6 | 50.5 | 56.7 | 56.0 | 60.0 |
| Subsidies | 3.3 | 3.8 | 4.7 | 5.7 | 5.6 | 5.5 | 5.1 |
| Grants | 17.2 | 20.3 | 24.1 | 28.4 | 34.3 | 34.1 | 38.4 |
| Debt interest | 6.5 | 7.6 | 9.8 | 11.9 | 13.8 | 13.7 | 14.4 |
| | | | | | | | |
| Current surplus | 0.5 | −1.3 | 1.0 | −1.6 | 0.8 | 0.4 | 1.7 |
| | | | | | | | |
| Capital receipts, total[1] | 1.5 | −0.3 | 2.2 | −0.2 | 2.6 | 2.1 | 3.1 |
| Capital expenditure, total | 6.6 | 6.6 | 7.5 | 8.2 | 7.1 | 7.0 | 7.6 |
| of which: | | | | | | | |
| Fixed investment | 4.7 | 4.7 | 5.4 | 5.6 | 4.4 | 4.3 | 4.8 |
| | | | | | | | |
| Financial deficit, total | 5.1 | 6.9 | 5.3 | 8.4 | 4.1 | 4.9 | 4.5 |
| of which: | | | | | | | |
| Central government | 3.4 | 5.1 | 2.8 | 6.5 | 5.1 | 6.1 | 5.8 |
| Local authorities | 1.7 | 1.7 | 2.5 | 1.9 | −1.0 | 1.2 | 1.2 |
| | | | | | | | |
| Memorandum items: | | | | | | | |
| PSBR, total | 5.6 | 9.2 | 9.9 | 13.2 | 8.8 | 10.6 | 9.5 |
| of which: | | | | | | | |
| Central government | 4.4 | 8.1 | 8.2 | 13.0 | 7.5 | 8.8 | 9.3 |
| Local authorities | 0.4 | 1.0 | 2.1 | 1.0 | 1.0 | 1.6 | 0.8 |
| Public corporations | 0.7 | 0.2 | −0.5 | −0.7 | 0.2 | 0.2 | −0.6 |

1.  Including current surplus.
*Sources:  Financial Statistics*, CSO; Financial Statement and Budget Report 1982-83, HMSO.

was running at an annual rate of about £6 billion compared wtih a £9½ billion Budget estimate. The shortfall on the central government financial deficit seems to be smaller. The shortfalls appear to be largely attributable to less borrowing by public corporations, to declining local authority investment and to delays in settling pay increases in parts of local government and in the health service. Lower inflation also contributed. Local authority underspending on certain items is considerable, notably on housing which is almost one-half of the budget estimates. Rapidly falling interest rates will also contribute to the decline in debt servicing charges in 1982/83; and largely reflecting the stronger than budgeted increase in oil prices, oil tax revenues are running at a rate of about £¾ billion over projection.

In the "Autumn Statement" on the state of the economy presented on 8th November, 1982, the Chancellor announced tax and expenditure measures[29] with the aim of correcting part of the shortfalls in the PSBR and thus stimulate somewhat the economy in view of the considerably weaker real and inflationary developments in

29.  For details see Calendar of Main Economic Events.

1982/83 than had been forecast at Budget time. The measures include a reduction of the NIS (National Insurance Surcharge paid by employers), partly offsetting increases in National Insurance contributions (paid by both employers and employees), a small decline in real social security benefits in the autumn of 1983 in order to take account of the unexpectedly substantial real growth in 1982/83 (arising from the sharp decline in inflation) and lastly, moderate reductions in planned expenditure in 1983/84 in cash largely explained by the lower inflation than initially forecast early in 1982. In addition, the Autumn Statement suggests that the retroactive NIS relief be deducted from employers' national insurance payments in the first three months of 1983 which, together with an increase in the rate of investment spending, may largely make good the shortfall in the PSBR in the first half of 1982/83. As a result, the authorities expect that the PSBR could be up to £9 billion in 1982/83 as a whole, which is £½ billion (or ¼ percentage point of GDP) less than budgeted. Moreover, the Autumn Statement indicates that an increase of expenditure and/or a reduction of tax revenues of about £1 billion is also required if the PSBR in 1983/84 is to be 2¾ per cent of GDP as envisaged in the MTFS.

Partly because public sector investment, especially local authority investment, may not adjust as quickly as the authorities would have wished, the GGFD may be lower than expected but still rise to about 2 per cent of GDP in 1982/83, while the PSBR will continue falling by almost ½ percentage point to around 3 per cent of GDP[30]. With real GDP growth still below potential, the increase in the GGFD as a per cent of GDP will be mainly due to automatic stabilisers. The impact of the cyclically adjusted budget change in 1982/83 may therefore be marginally restrictive or at best broadly neutral[31] compared with strong contraction in earlier years. However, taking into account the lagged effects from the significant tightening in 1981/82, the overall budgetary impact is estimated by the Secretariat to be restrictive in 1982/83 as well. The United Kingdom authorities believe that the stance of fiscal policy is not well expressed by the cyclically adjusted PSBR, nor indeed by any single measure. Other factors, including the rate of inflation, and the consequences for interest rates, are also relevant in judging the stance of fiscal policy[32]. Roughly in line with the projected sharper decline in inflation, the Autumn Statement has revised downwards the earlier forecasts in the 1982/83 Budget regarding government expenditure in 1983/84 and government receipts so that (including the £1 billion fiscal adjustment) both the GGBR and the PSBR are officially projected to be 2¾ per cent of GDP in 1983/84, much as had been estimated under the Medium-Term Financial Strategy in the Budget of last March.

The fiscal tightening in the last two years is in line with the Government's medium-term anti-inflationary policy, which considers that the significant rise in the size of the public sector in the 1970s was a major cause of the present difficult economic situation which, unless reversed, would continue inhibiting the resumption of self-sustained growth. The following few paragraphs describe the fiscal and expenditure trends since the late 1960s followed by a brief review of the medium-term government expenditure plans, 1981/82 to 1983/84, during which period the authorities expect to bring about most of the desired fiscal adjustments.

As in most other OECD countries, both government expenditure and borrowing recorded substantial real growth during the first half of the 1970s; the former from

30. In the first eight months of 1982/83 the PSBR was still running below £7 billion, annual rate, suggesting that its level in the financial year as a whole may be about £8 billion.

31. After taking into account that most of the delayed tax payments will be recovered in 1982/83 thus lowering the GGFD by about ½ per cent of GDP, the underlying change in the budgetary stance is broadly neutral.

32. The authorities' position is presented in: HM Treasury, *Economic Progress Report*, No. 144 of April 1982: "The Budget Balance; measurement and policy".

## Table 8. Longer-run fiscal trends
### As a per cent of GDP

| | 1969/ 1970 | 1970/ 1971 | 1971/ 1972 | 1972/ 1973 | 1973/ 1974 | 1974/ 1975 | 1975/ 1976 | 1976/ 1977 | 1977/ 1978 | 1978/ 1979 | 1979/ 1980 | 1980/ 1981 | 1981/ 1982 |
|---|---|---|---|---|---|---|---|---|---|---|---|---|---|
| **Public expenditure** | | | | | | | | | | | | | |
| General government, total | 40.8[1] | 40.9[1] | 41.7 | 41.5 | 43.4 | 48.5 | 48.8 | 46.4 | 42.5 | 43.8 | 44.1 | 46.5 | 47.1 |
| Current expenditure | 32.0[1] | 32.1[1] | 32.6 | 32.9 | 34.8 | 38.5 | 39.6 | 39.5 | 38.2 | 38.6 | 39.0 | 41.4 | 43.5 |
| Final consumption | 17.2[1] | 17.6[1] | 18.0 | 18.1 | 18.8 | 20.7 | 21.7 | 21.3 | 20.2 | 19.9 | 20.0 | 21.7 | 22.3 |
| Transfers and subsidies | 14.8[1] | 14.5[1] | 14.6 | 14.8 | 16.0 | 17.8 | 17.9 | 18.2 | 18.0 | 18.7 | 19.0 | 19.7 | 21.1 |
| Capital expenditure | 6.7[1] | 6.4[1] | 5.9 | 5.9 | 6.8 | 6.5 | 6.0 | 5.4 | 4.4 | 3.9 | 3.7 | 3.5 | 2.8 |
| Net lending | 2.2[1] | 2.4[1] | 2.7 | 2.7 | 1.8 | 3.5 | 3.2 | 1.5 | -0.1 | 1.3 | 1.4 | 1.6 | 1.2 |
| Central government | | | | | | | 33.5 | 32.2 | 30.1 | 31.7 | 31.8 | 33.8 | 35.4 |
| Local authorities | | | | | | | 15.3 | 14.1 | 12.5 | 12.1 | 12.3 | 12.7 | 12.0 |
| **Public expenditure programmes** | | | | | | | | | | | | | |
| General government adjusted | | | | | | | 43.2 | 40.7 | 37.4 | 38.3 | 38.1 | 39.9 | 40.8 |
| Certain public corporations | | | | | | | 0.9 | 0.8 | 0.7 | 0.6 | 0.6 | 0.6 | 0.6 |
| Nationalised industries' market and overseas borrowing | | | | | | | 0.5 | 1.0 | 0.6 | 0.3 | -0.1 | -0.2 | 0.2 |
| *Less:* Special sales of assets | | | | | | | | | -0.3 | — | -0.5 | -0.2 | 0.0 |
| Planning total (White Paper basis) | | | 37.2 | 38.0 | 39.7 | 44.6 | 44.5 | 42.5 | 38.4 | 39.0 | 38.1 | 40.2 | 41.6 |
| Public sector interest payments | 4.4 | 4.1 | 3.9 | 3.8 | 4.5 | 4.8 | 4.6 | 5.0 | 4.8 | 4.8 | 5.2 | 5.4 | 5.8 |
| General government interest payments | 4.1 | 3.8 | 3.7 | 3.6 | 4.1 | 4.2 | 4.2 | 4.4 | 4.3 | 4.5 | 4.8 | 5.1 | 5.4 |
| **Financial deficits, total** | -1.5 | 1.0 | 1.2 | 3.0 | 4.7 | 6.7 | 7.5 | 5.8 | 4.3 | 4.8 | 3.7 | 4.6 | 2.4 |
| General government | -2.0[1] | -3.1[1] | -0.5 | -0.5 | 3.6 | 4.5 | 5.1 | 4.5 | 3.5 | 4.1 | 2.6 | 3.6 | 1.8 |
| Central government | -4.6[1] | -5.6[1] | -2.5 | 2.3 | 0.3 | 1.4 | 3.1 | 2.6 | 2.3 | 3.0 | 1.4 | 2.8 | 2.0 |
| Local authorities | 2.6[1] | 2.5[1] | 2.0 | 2.3 | 3.3 | 3.1 | 2.0 | 1.9 | 1.1 | 1.0 | 1.2 | 0.8 | -0.2 |
| Public corporations | 1.1[1] | 1.6[1] | 1.7 | 1.2 | 1.1 | 2.4 | 2.4 | 1.3 | 0.8 | 0.8 | 1.1 | 1.0 | 0.6 |
| **PSBR, total** | -1.1 | 1.6 | 1.7 | 3.8 | 6.1 | 9.1 | 9.6 | 6.6 | 3.7 | 5.4 | 4.9 | 5.7 | 3.4 |
| General government | -1.2 | 1.1 | 2.0 | 3.8 | 5.1 | 8.3 | 9.1 | 5.7 | 3.3 | 5.3 | 5.1 | 6.0 | 3.4 |
| Central government | -2.3 | — | 1.0 | 2.9 | 3.0 | 5.8 | 8.0 | 4.6 | 2.9 | 4.8 | 4.0 | 5.6 | 3.0 |
| Local authorities | 1.1 | 1.1 | 1.0 | 0.9 | 2.2 | 2.5 | 1.2 | 1.1 | 0.3 | 0.5 | 1.0 | 0.4 | 0.4 |
| Public corporations | 0.1 | 0.5 | -0.3 | — | 0.9 | 0.8 | 0.5 | 0.9 | 0.5 | 0.2 | -0.2 | -0.3 | 0.1 |
| **General government, total receipts** | 40.8 | 41.1 | 41.6 | 37.0 | 38.0 | 40.6 | 40.6 | 40.4 | 39.2 | 38.7 | 40.1 | 41.3 | 44.5 |
| Current | 42.2 | 39.9 | 37.8 | 35.8 | 36.7 | 39.5 | 39.8 | 39.8 | 38.6 | 38.1 | 39.5 | 40.7 | 43.8 |
| *Of which:* Total taxes | 30.9 | 30.8 | 28.8 | 26.7 | 26.9 | 28.9 | 29.1 | 28.7 | 27.8 | 27.9 | 29.3 | 30.0 | 32.7 |
| National insurance contributions | 5.0 | 5.1 | 5.1 | 5.3 | 5.6 | 6.1 | 6.5 | 6.9 | 6.5 | 6.1 | 5.9 | 6.2 | 6.5 |
| Capital | 1.2 | 1.2 | 1.2 | 1.2 | 1.3 | 1.1 | 0.8 | 0.7 | 0.6 | 0.6 | 0.6 | 0.6 | 0.7 |

1. Calendar year, 1969 and 1970 respectively.
*Sources: Financial Statistics, CSO; National Income and Expenditure, CSO (1967-1977).*

about 40 per cent of GDP in the late 1960s to 48¾ per cent in 1975/76[33] (Table 8). About half of the increase was due to the growing economic slack which was reflected in a marked increase of subsidies and transfers and about half reflected the rise of government consumption as both real earnings of government employees and government employment rose considerably over this period[34]. Contrary to expenditure, total government receipts and taxes remained relatively stable, with the cyclical effects about offset by discretionary changes.

After the record public sector deficits in 1975/76, the authorities took important measures to reduce them, despite the continuously growing demand-determined expenditure and unfavourable effects on revenues. As Table 8 shows, the GGFD and the PSBR declined to 1¾ per cent and 3½ per cent of GDP respectively in 1981/82, which is the trough of the most severe post-war recession. This was achieved by a substantial rise in total government revenue (concentrated in the last two years). This mainly reflected an increase in taxes (including national insurance contributions) which reached nearly 40 per cent of GDP in 1981/82 compared with 35 per cent on average during the second half of the 1970s. About half of the increase in taxes is due to North Sea oil taxes – first levied in 1979 – which rose to just over 2 per cent of GDP in 1981/82. Indirect taxes also increased over the last two years reflecting the increase in the VAT in 1979/80 in an effort to shift part of the tax burden from incomes on to expenditure with the declared aim of improving the supply side of the economy by rewarding initiative and work. Total government expenditure remained broadly stable between 1975/76 and 1981/82 due to a marked fall in government fixed investment to 1¾ per cent of GDP in 1981/82 or just over one-third the average rate in the first half of the 1970s. This was offset by continuing growth of current expenditure in real terms; notably due to rising unemployment and real social benefits, current grants to households increased steadily reaching 13 per cent of GDP in 1981/82, or 2½ percentage points higher than in the previous trough in 1975/76.

Reflecting a marked slowdown in the growth of real average earnings and employment[35], government consumption declined a little up to 1979/80 before reaching 22¼ per cent of GDP in 1981/82, which is slightly above that of the previous trough in 1975/76 (Table 8). This was almost exclusively due to a marked rise in average earnings in the general government sector largely reflecting the recommendations of the Clegg Commission's report on public sector pay[36]. On the other hand, the long-term upward trend in employment in the government sector has been reversed, with employment falling in both central and local government[37]. The increase in nominal interest payments was relatively small when seen against the successive high public sector

33.   General government expenditure excluding financial transactions (i.e. lending and net acquisition of financial assets) rose from 38½ per cent of GDP in the late 1960s to 45½ per cent in 1975/76.

34.   The annual rate of growth of average earnings in the public sector (including public corporations) was 17¼ per cent between 1969 and 1975 and in general government nearly 17 per cent compared with 16 per cent in the private sector. At the same time, the annual rate of growth of employment in government sectors was 3 per cent over this period compared with a small decline in the private sector.

35.   The annual rate of growth of average earnings in government decelerated to 11 per cent between 1975/76 and 1979/80 (compared with an annual rate of 15 per cent in the private sector) with employment growth slowing down to ¾ per cent, annual rate, over the same period.

36.   The Clegg Commission's recommendations (which were based amongst other criteria on comparability with the private sector) were almost fully applied leading to fairly big increases in government pay of 21 per cent on average in the two years to 1981 compared with 16½ per cent in the private sector. Subsequently, certain of the Commission's recommendations for such large pay increases were considered unfounded and over the last year and a half the authorities have been trying to correct some of these excessive rises.

37.   Between spring 1979 and early 1982, Civil Service employment was reduced by 60 000 (8 per cent) and local authorities' manpower by over 70 000 (3 per cent). These reductions were partly offset by an increase of 40 000 (5 per cent) in manpower in the National Health Service.

deficits and especially the big rise in nominal interest rates since the mid-1970s[38]. This is explained by the significant erosion of public sector debt due to the acceleration of inflation since the early 1970s; the market value of public sector net debt fell from about two-thirds of GDP in 1970 to a little over one-third in the early 1980s[39].

Financial transactions – namely net sales of assets and a fall in government lending to the private sector and to overseas – more than offset the small rise in government expenditure so that total government expenditure including financial transactions fell by nearly 1½ percentage points after 1975/76 to 47¼ per cent of GDP in 1981/82. However, this is still significantly above the average level of the early 1970s (41½ per cent of GDP) before the first oil crisis and higher than the average level of the 1970s (44¾ per cent) and more than can be explained by the demand-determined expenditure components caused by the growing slack, which suggests a rising structural component.

The Government's Expenditure Plans to 1984/85[40], which are for the first time presented in cash terms instead of cost (volume) terms, project a significant slowdown in the rate of growth of nominal public sector expenditure beginning in 1982/83; the annual rate of growth is set at 6½ per cent in the three years to 1984/85 compared with 17¼ per cent over the previous three years. This slowdown reflects both price and volume changes. An important factor is the Government's determination to continue reducing the number of people working in general government and keeping under control the growth in average earnings in the public sector. Government grants and lending to nationalised industries are also expected to decline significantly between 1981/82 and 1984/85. Similarly, special sales of assets (including company shares) are projected to continue at an important rate over the medium term thus reducing the rate of increase of total planned public expenditure.

Another factor which will help to contain the growth in public expenditure is a substantial slowdown in interest payments which apparently is based on the assumption of a marked decline in nominal interest rates[41] over the projection period. Similarly, the growth in demand-determined expenditure items (such as unemployment benefits, pensions, etc.) are expected to decelerate in cash terms but probably not in volume given the rise in the total of unemployment and other related benefits over this period. On the basis first, of a small real decline in total government expenditure by 1984/85 to about its average level of the 1970s as a per cent of GDP and, secondly of broadly stable real government receipts, the PSBR is forecast to decline further over the next three years to less than 2 per cent of GDP by 1984/85, and the GGFD to somewhat less than that. On the assumption of a small recovery in activity broadly in line or somewhat above potential growth, these deficits imply continuing tight fiscal posture over the medium term accompanied by some release of resources to the private sector.

*Monetary policy*

The perception of monetary policy and its role have changed in several respects in recent years. Greater recognition is now given to the two-way relationship between

38.   The yield of Treasury Bills was around 11 per cent in 1975 and 15½ per cent in 1981. The rise in long-term gilt-edged stock was smaller.
39.   See *Bank of England Quarterly Bulletin,* June 1982, pp. 239-242 for a full analysis of the effects of inflation on the real value of public debt.
40.   Cmnd 8494 – I and II, March 1982, HMSO, London.
41.   Gross (net) interest payments are forecast to increase at an annual rate of 4½ per cent (6½ per cent) in the three years to 1984/85 compared with 20 per cent (37½ per cent) over the previous three years. However, if interest rates continue to decline as in the recent period, interest payments may be broadly stable in the next two years.

monetary changes on the one hand and changes in inflation and/or in real variables on the other hand. In association with this, there is also much greater uncertainty regarding the lag structure of these relationships and the first round perverse effects that certain policy changes may cause, especially in times of recession[42]. Moreover, the control of the

Diagram 8. **Interest rates**

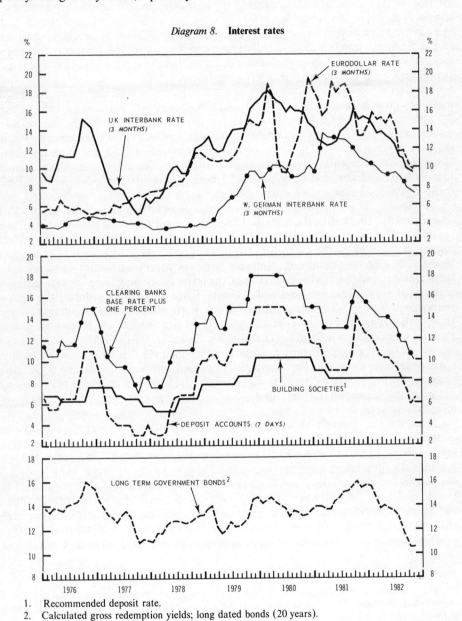

1. Recommended deposit rate.
2. Calculated gross redemption yields; long dated bonds (20 years).

*Sources: Financial Statistics;* Bank of England, *Quarterly Bulletin* and OECD, Secretariat estimates.

42. An important rise in interest rates instead of curbing demand for credit may in the beginning, by increasing the debt servicing charges and by reducing real demand, aggravate significantly cash-flow position of companies forcing them to increase their demand for credit.

31

monetary aggregates, which is officially designated to reflect overall monetary conditions (as was the case for sterling M3), has proven difficult and not always very effective insofar as substitute financial instruments can be created. Though the latter may not directly influence the stated monetary aggregate, thus giving for a time the impression that monetary developments are in the desired direction, they can have a considerable impact on overall financial and monetary conditions, which then may move in a different direction to the monetary target. Similarly, important structural changes[43] in the financial markets and the distortions arising from the frequent changes in monetary regulations, instruments and techniques[44] over the last decade have increased the difficulties in interpreting monetary conditions.

Reflecting greater flexibility in monetary management, the target ranges of monetary growth were set in the March 1982 Budget at 8-12 per cent for 1982/83 and 7-11 per cent for 1983/84, somewhat higher than indicated earlier. In line with the disinflationary role assigned to monetary variables, a projection of 6-10 per cent was, for the first time, fixed for 1984/85. Moreover, recognising that no single monetary aggregate can encapsulate overall monetary conditions, the target range was extended to include (in addition to sterling-M3) M1 (money supply narrowly defined) and PSL2 (private sector liquidity more widely defined[45]).

Following the abolition of the "supplementary special deposit scheme" (the Corset) which aimed at controlling the growth of deposits[46], monetary policy mainly operates on the demand for money and credit via the PSBR and interest rates, especially short-term interest rates on which the authorities (through open market operations) have a greater leverage than on long-term rates. Interest rate policy has traditionally been geared to both domestic and external considerations, the latter continuing to be important in view of the volatility of exchange rates and of United States interest rates during the last two years. Accordingly, short-term interest rates have often moved in sympathy with Euro-dollar interest rates. After reaching a high in late October 1981, nominal interest rates have declined considerably (Diagram 8). However, the fall in the rate of inflation has meant that real interest rates have been maintained at a fairly high positive level for almost eighteen months. The historically high real interest rates during a period of recession had no doubt a considerable restrictive impact with its direct effects mostly visible on investment on the real side and on the exchange rate, which in turn negatively affected competitiveness and growth.

Despite the marked slowdown in inflation, continuing sluggish activity and improved financial conditions in the company sector, bank lending in sterling to the private sector surged to about £11½ billion over the year to mid-1982 compared with less than £8 billion during the previous year. There was a strong rise in bank lending to the personal sector for house purchases to almost £4 billion (£3 billion more than in the year to mid-1981). A significant part of this acceleration reflected a structural change in the financial markets, the banks increasing their activities in mortgage finance; their share in total lending for house purchases rose from about 7 per cent during the three years to 1980 to one-fourth in 1981 and to more than one-third in the first half of 1982

---

43. Capital issues accounted for about 40 per cent of company borrowing (excluding capital issues) in the years up to the early 1970s: since then this figure has fallen to less than 15 per cent on average (20 per cent in 1981).

44. Some of the most recent changes are described in the OECD Economic Survey of the United Kingdom, July 1981, page 44 and in the monetary section of earlier Surveys.

45. PSL2 includes certain deposits with savings institutions which are excluded from sterling M3 (the latter only includes bank deposits). Certain shares and deposits with building societies are the largest single component of PSL2 other than bank deposits.

46. Banks recording faster rates of growth of deposits than had been authorised were penalised by placing non-interest bearing deposits with the Bank of England at progressively higher rates.

## Table 9. Monetary aggregates
### Seasonally adjusted, annual rate

| | 1978 | 1979 | 1980 | 1981 | 1981 II | I | Q2 | July 1982 | August | Sept. | Oct. |
|---|---|---|---|---|---|---|---|---|---|---|---|
| **Components of monetary expansion[1] (£ billion)** | | | | | | | | | | | |
| a) Public sector borrowing requirement | 8.4 | 12.6 | 12.2 | 10.6 | 6.6 | 1.4 | 6.2 | -5.8 | 2.8 | -11.0 | 24.0 |
| b) Purchases of public sector debt by private sector[2] | 6.0 | 10.9 | 9.5 | 11.2 | 9.0 | 8.4 | 3.7 | | | | |
| c) Lending in sterling | 4.7 | 8.6 | 10.0 | 11.3 | 16.5 | 18.4 | 13.5 | 18.3 | 15.7 | 24.3 | 21.6 |
| d) Domestic counterparts | 7.0 | 10.3 | 12.8 | 10.8 | 14.0 | 11.4 | 16.0 | 12.4 | 18.5 | 13.4 | 24.7 |
| e) External finance | 0.7 | -3.1 | -0.5 | 0.2 | -2.2 | -2.6 | -5.4 | -8.0 | -2.3 | 2.4 | -3.3 |
| f) Net non-deposit liabilities | -0.9 | -0.6 | -1.4 | -1.6 | -1.7 | -1.4 | -2.2 | 3.9 | -1.8 | -3.5 | -3.2 |
| g) Sterling M3 | 6.8 | 6.6 | 10.9 | 9.4 | 10.1 | 7.5 | 8.4 | 8.3 | 14.4 | 12.3 | 18.2 |
| **Bank lending[3] (£ billion)** | | | | | | | | | | | |
| To private sector, total | 5.7 | 9.5 | 10.9 | 11.5 | 15.4 | 13.5 | 17.7 | 4.8 | 25.1 | 13.5 | 19.0 |
| sterling | 4.7 | 8.6 | 9.6 | 8.8 | 10.7 | 12.0 | 16.9 | 5.5 | 19.8 | 13.5 | 19.0 |
| other currencies | 1.0 | 0.9 | 1.3 | 2.8 | 4.7 | 1.5 | 0.8 | -0.7 | 5.3 | 0.0 | 0.0 |
| To overseas sector, total | 20.9 | 30.4 | 33.8 | 41.6 | 46.8 | 19.2 | -4.0 | 69.3 | 89.7 | 25.5 | 34.8 |
| sterling | 1.1 | — | 2.8 | 3.2 | 3.2 | 2.7 | -0.2 | 4.0 | 5.9 | 3.9 | 9.7 |
| other currencies | 19.9 | 30.4 | 31.0 | 38.4 | 43.5 | 16.5 | -3.8 | 65.3 | 83.8 | 21.6 | 25.1 |
| **Total borrowing (£ billion) n.s.a.** | | | | | | | | | | | |
| Personal sector, total | 8.2 | 10.9 | 11.0 | 14.4 | 15.1 | 16.4 | 18.0 | | | | |
| of which: for house purchase, total | 5.5 | 6.6 | 7.4 | 9.8 | 10.6 | 12.0 | 14.0 | | | | |
| of which: from banks | 0.3 | 0.6 | 0.5 | 2.5 | 3.7 | 4.5 | 5.1 | | | | |
| Industrial and commercial companies, total | 4.8 | 6.9 | 10.7 | 10.9 | 17.3 | 11.8 | 5.7 | | | | |
| of which: from banks | 2.9 | 4.9 | 6.8 | 4.5 | 7.7 | 3.0 | 7.8 | | | | |
| other loans and mortgages | 0.4 | 0.7 | 0.7 | 3.8 | 6.9 | 7.1 | -2.6 | | | | |
| capital issues | 0.8 | 0.9 | 1.3 | 1.7 | 2.3 | 1.1 | 1.6 | | | | |
| **Monetary aggregates (percentage changes)[1]** | | | | | | | | *Change over previous six months (annual rate)* | | | |
| Narrowly defined M1 | 16.7 | 9.3 | 4.0 | 9.2 | 3.3 | 10.3 | 10.5 | 5.1 | 8.1 | 12.4 | 19.0 |
| Broadly defined M3 | 15.1 | 12.5 | 19.1 | 17.9 | 14.7 | 10.0 | 10.0 | 11.8 | 13.7 | 13.2 | 14.2 |
| Sterling M3[5] | 15.2 | 12.9 | 19.0 | 13.4 | 13.8 | 7.7 | 8.5 | 8.0 | 10.9 | 12.1 | 14.7 |
| Savings institutions, deposits and securities | 14.3 | 10.4 | 9.6 | 11.6 | 3.9 | 9.2 | 4.8 | 6.7 | 4.1 | 4.0 | 4.8 |
| Private sector liquidity, widely defined, PSL2 | 14.9 | 13.6 | 13.5 | 11.5 | 9.2 | 8.9 | 6.4 | 6.8 | 7.7 | 8.7 | 9.4 |

1. The relationship between the lines is: a—b+c=d, d—e—f=g.
2. Excluding bank purchases.
3. Excluding Bank of England purchases of commercial bills.
4. The annual percentage changes are based on the sum of calendar quarter changes during the year as a percentage of the money stock outstanding at the end of the previous year. The quarterly figures relate to seasonally adjusted amounts outstanding at the end of each quarter.
5. Sterling M3 is equal to M3 excluding United Kingdom residents' deposits in other currencies.
*Sources: Financial statistics*, CSO.

(mainly at the expense of building societies)[47]. There was also an increase in bank loans to unincorporated business, and it appears that a small part of bank lending for house purchases may have been deflected to consumption. Bank lending to industrial and commercial companies also rose – especially in late 1981 and early 1982 – to pay tax arrears and probably to a lesser extent to restore more normal liquidity conditions.

Credit expansion to the domestic sectors continued to be substantial after June 1982[48] (around £16 billion, annual rate up to November), possibly because of renewed pressure on private sector liquidity stemming from weakening activity. The sharp decline in inflation may have increased companies' interest burden in real terms. Also, the abolition of hire purchase controls probably led to an upturn in demand from credit by households. Lastly, partly because of the delays in putting into effect their commitment to slow down credit expansion for housing, the high rate of bank lending for housing seems to have been maintained up to around the end of 1982. Building societies' mortgage lending also accelerated in the second half of the year.

The strong demand for credit combined with "over-funding"[49], which curbed the growth of private sector deposits with banks and other financial intermediaries, led at times to severe squeezes on the banks' cash position. Given the near-depletion of Treasury bills held by banks[50], the Bank of England provided the necessary cash by outright purchases of commercial bills[51] and to a lesser extent through the repurchase agreements. This injection of cash through the banks to the financial market contributed importantly in smoothing out short-term interest rate movements and in allowing them to maintain their downward trend in order not to aggravate the recessionary tendencies in the economy. Accordingly, the effects of "over-funding" on the overall liquidity of the economy were broadly neutralised. However, overfunding, together with high real interest rates prevailing at the long end of the market made companies rely increasingly on banks' short-term credit.

The falling PSBR coupled with overfunding (which began in early 1981 and continued up to last May) exerted a strong contractionary effect on the growth of sterling-M3 in the year to mid-1982. Similarly, reflecting the continuing large private sector net capital outflows, foreign transactions exerted a restrictive impact over this period. These contractionary elements mitigated the strong expansionary effects on monetary growth of the surge in bank lending to the private sector. Thus, after rising considerably above the target of 6-10 per cent growth rate (fixed in the 1981 Budget) up to late 1981[52], the growth of sterling-M3 was brought to less than 10 per cent during the first half of 1982. The annual rate of growth of sterling M3 accelerated to about 12 per cent during the second half-year, giving an overall growth since last February of just over 11 per cent, annual rate, which is within the target range set early in 1982. To the extent that the acceleration in the second half-year is partially due to once-for-all effects such as the abolition of hire purchase controls, and higher borrowing by companies

47. Up to 1980, building societies accounted for some four-fifths of private sector mortgage finance.

48. Credit expansion in sterling to the domestic sectors was about £12¼ billion in 1981/82.

49. Overfunding occurs when the public sector deficit is more than covered by direct non-bank private sector purchases of gilt-edged paper.

50. The ratio of Treasury bills held by banks to their total sterling assets fell from about 6 per cent in the mid-1970s to less than 1 per cent over the last year.

51. The Bank's holdings of commercial (mainly banks) bills rose from £3½ billion in March 1981 to about £8½ billion in August 1982, thereby largely offsetting the contractionary impact from "over funding".

52. The growth of sterling M3 was distorted by the Civil Service dispute. The delays in tax collection left companies with more liquidity than they may have normally wished to hold, which they deposited with banks thus inflating money supply.

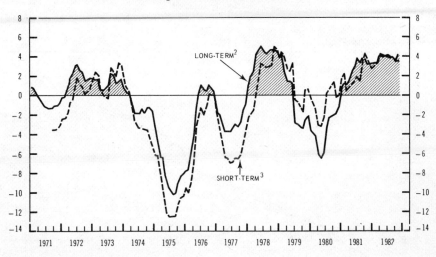

*Diagram 9.* **Real interest rates[1]**

1. Interest rates divided by the retail price index.
2. Long dated bonds (20 years).
3. Clearing banks base rate plus one per cent.

*Source:* OECD, Secretariat estimates.

reflecting the unexpected weaker activity in the second half-year, it does not suggest excessive underlying monetary growth.

The wider measure of private sector liquidity – notably PSL2 which is a better indicator of total liquidity conditions – has been rising at a slower rate than sterling M3 since 1980[53], which together with the downward trend in the PSBR suggest that overall financial and monetary developments are within the limits set out in the 1982/83 Budget. The important divergence in the growth rates of sterling-M3 and of PSL2 reflects the shift in financial intermediation away from savings' institutions and in favour of banks[54]. The marked acceleration in the growth of M1 (money supply narrowly defined) since June (Table 9) reflects to a large extent the decline in nominal interest rates which made holding of cash or nearly liquid deposits more attractive. It may also indicate that companies facing short-term liquidity shortages prefer to hold liquid assets. Another interesting feature is the sharp decline in the velocity of circulation over the last two years to early 1982, when it reached the lowest level since 1974 suggesting that the monetary base could support a rapid recovery without causing major strains in financial markets.

53. The annual rate of growth of PSL2 was about 9 per cent between February and December 1982.
54. In the summer, the banks made clear their intention of stemming the excessive growth of house lending and hence a convergence in the growth rates of sterling-M3 and PSL2 seems probable over the near future. The big differences in the growth rates between sterling-M3 and M3 are due to a valuation effect.

### Diagram 10. Money supply and liquidity trends
Seasonally adjusted

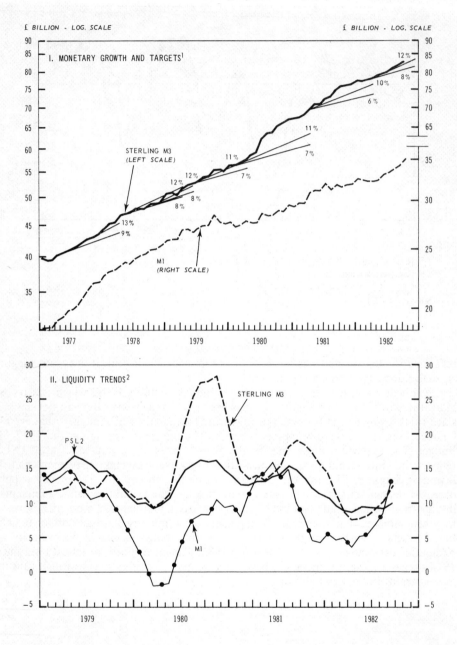

£ BILLION - LOG. SCALE

£ BILLION - LOG. SCALE

I. MONETARY GROWTH AND TARGETS[1]

STERLING M3
(LEFT SCALE)

M1
(RIGHT SCALE)

1977 1978 1979 1980 1981 1982

II. LIQUIDITY TRENDS[2]

PSL2

STERLING M3

M1

1979 1980 1981 1982

1. The semi-log. scale was used for both items but for the sake of presentation the bottom part was shifted upwards and shown as a right scale.
2. Three month moving average, percentage changes over six months earlier at annual rate.
*Sources:* Bank of England, *Quarterly Bulletin* and *Financial Statistics.*

# III. SHORT-TERM PROSPECTS[55]

The projections summarised in Table 11 and discussed below are subject to greater uncertainty than usual:

*i)* The evaluation of external demand, influenced by the timing and strength of the recovery in the OECD, may be adversely affected by increasing protectionist pressures and financial restrictions in many developing countries.

*ii)* The possible trends in interest rates are difficult to assess, being heavily dependent on developments in international markets.

*iii)* The current indicators shown in Table 10 present a more mixed picture than is normally the case.

### Table 10. Recent conjunctural indicators

| | 1980 | 1981 | 1982 I | Q2 | Q3 | Sept. | Oct. | Nov. |
|---|---|---|---|---|---|---|---|---|
| | | | (Index 1981=100) | | | | | |
| GDP f.c. output based | 102.5 | 100 | 100.3 | 100.4 | 100.8 | | | |
| GDP m.p. compromise | 102.3 | 100 | 100.6 | 100.2 | 100.7 | | | |
| Private consumption | 99.6 | 100 | 100.0 | 99.8 | 101.5 | | | |
| Industrial production | 105.4 | 100 | 100.5 | 100.7 | 101.3 | 101.5 | 101.1 | |
| Manufacturing production | 106.7 | 100 | 99.7 | 99.4 | 98.9 | 99.1 | 98.3 | |
| Volume retail sales | 98.9 | 100 | 100.8 | 100.6 | 103.0 | 103.4 | 103.5 | 103.7 |
| Employment (G.B.) | | | | | | | | |
|   Production industries | 110.1 | 100 | 95.1 | 94.6 | 93.1 | 92.8 | 92.5 | |
|   Manufacturing | 110.9 | 100 | 95.5 | 94.8 | 93.3 | 92.9 | 92.6 | |
| Unemployment rate[1] | (6.8) | (10.6) | (11.9) | (12.0) | (12.5) | (12.7) | | |
| Vacancies (thousand) | (143) | (97) | (110) | (107) | (111) | (114.6) | (120.3) | (111.1) |
| Imports of goods (volume)[2] | 98.5 | 100 | 106.5 | 109.2 | 105.5 | 107.6 | 105.5 | 105.9 |
| Exports of goods (volume)[2] | 103.1 | 100 | 100.7 | 102.6 | 95.9 | 102.1 | 98.0 | 102.3 |
| | Annual percentage rate of change from previous period | | | Percentage change from six months earlier (annual rate) | | | | |
| Retail prices (excluding seasonal food) | 18.4 | 11.9 | 8.8 | 9.0 | 8.5 | 7.7 | 4.7 | 4.5 |
| Average earnings | 20.7 | 12.9 | 7.5 | 7.8 | 10.2 | 6.0 | 7.8 | |
| | $US billion, annual rates | | | | | | | |
| Imports | 107.4 | 96.6 | 96.3 | 97.0 | 91.5 | 92.5 | 90.5 | 7.4 |
| Exports | 110.2 | 102.7 | 97.9 | 97.9 | 94.3 | 97.8 | 95.9 | 96.6 |
| Trade balance | 2.8 | 6.1 | 1.6 | 0.7 | 2.8 | 5.3 | 5.3 | 9.2 |
|   *of which:* Oil | 0.6 | 6.1 | 5.8 | 6.4 | 8.7 | 7.7 | 10.1 | 9.9 |
| Current balance | 7.1 | 12.1 | 5.9 | 6.3 | 6.9 | 9.4 | 10.0 | 11.4 |

1. United Kingdom, excluding school leavers, as a percentage of total employees (old basis: see footnotes in table 2).
2. Excluding oil.
*Sources: Economic Trends, Department of Employment Gazette* and *Monthly Review of External Trade Statistics.*

55. The projections shown here are OECD projections and differ from those published in the OECD *Economic Outlook* No. 32 of December 1982. The present projections take into account the revised national accounts data and incorporate the 10 per cent effective depreciation of sterling between early November 1982 and early January 1983.

The assumptions underlying the forecast are that world trade will recover gradually to a rate of growth of between 4 and 5 per cent in the first half of 1984, that given rising unemployment, the fall in inflation and the policy of limiting salary rises in the public sector, the underlying growth of average earnings will decelerate to around 6½ per cent by mid-1984 and that real interest rates will be marginally reduced. In addition, unchanged exchange[56] rates and policies are also assumed. The latter assumption incorporates some easing of fiscal policy in conformity with the MTFS projections and the Autumn Statement. On this basis, and with a continuing fall in employment, labour costs are expected to be rising at an annual rate of about 4½ per cent in the year to mid-1984, which is the lowest since 1969. By the first half of 1984, the private consumption deflator[57] is projected to fall to about 6 per cent after allowing for the strong acceleration in the rise in import prices (due to the sharp fall in the sterling effective rate in the last two months of 1982) and a modest recovery in profits.

Real take-home pay is expected to begin rising again in the second half of 1982, which with some recovery in self-employment income and dividends and rising real transfers to households[58] should give a moderate growth of real disposable income

Table 11.  **Short-term prospects**
Annual percentage change from previous period

| | 1981 | 1982 | 1983 | 1982 II | 1983 I | 1983 II | 1984 I |
|---|---|---|---|---|---|---|---|
| Private consumption | 0.4 | 1 | 1¼ | 3½ | ½ | ½ | 1 |
| Government consumption | 0.0 | 1¾ | 1¼ | 2¾ | ½ | 1 | 1 |
| Fixed investment | −8.2 | 2½ | ¾ | ¾ | −½ | 3 | 2¾ |
| Public | −17.6 | −4¾ | 4¼ | 4¼ | 4¼ | 4¾ | 5¼ |
| Private | −3.8 | 5½ | −½ | −½ | −2¼ | 2½ | 1¾ |
| Final domestic demand | −1.2 | 1¼ | 1 | 3 | ¼ | 1 | 1¼ |
| Stockbuilding¹ | −0.3 | 1 | ¾ | −2 | 2 | 1 | ½ |
| Compromise adjustment¹ | −0.2 | −¼ | 0 | ½ | −¼ | 0 | ½ |
| Total domestic demand | −1.6 | 2 | 1¾ | 1½ | 2 | 2 | 2 |
| Exports | −2.2 | −¼ | 1¾ | −3 | 3½ | 3¼ | 3¾ |
| Imports | −0.3 | 4¼ | 3 | −¾ | 4 | 4½ | 4½ |
| Real foreign balance¹ | −0.5 | −1¼ | −½ | −½ | −¼ | −½ | −½ |
| GDP at market prices | −2.2 | ¾ | 1½ | 1 | 1¾ | 1½ | 1¾ |
| *Memorandum items:* | | | | | | | |
| Real personal disposable income | −1.9 | −2¼ | ½ | −1¼ | 1 | 1 | ¾ |
| Personal savings rate | 13.4 | 10¾ | 10 | 9½ | 9¾ | 10 | 10 |
| Private consumption deflator | 10.9 | 8 | 6¼ | 6 | 6¼ | 6 | 6 |
| Manufacturing production | −6.4 | −¼ | 0 | −2½ | ¼ | 1¼ | 1½ |
| Employees in employment | −4.5 | −3 | −2 | −3¼ | −2 | −1 | −¼ |
| Unemployment rate² | 11.3 | 13 | 14¼ | 13½ | 14 | 4½ | 14½ |
| Current balance of payments ($ US billion, annual rate) | 12.1 | 7¼ | 4½ | | | | |

1.  Change as a per cent of GDP in the previous period.
2.  United Kingdom, including school leavers as a per cent of total employees.
*Sources: Economic Trends,* CSO and OECD.

56.  The effective exchange rate is assumed to remain constant at the level of the first week of 1983.
57.  Implicit price consumption deflator on a national accounts basis, which has a wider coverage than the retail price index.
58.  The small reduction in real social security benefits per recipient from November 1983 will be more than offset by the increase in unemployment and the increase of other categories (including retired people) receiving social security benefits.

during the projection period. Falling inflation and the shift in the composition of household income in favour of wages and salaries and notably of government transfers to unemployed, pensioners and other low-income groups (which have an above average marginal propensity to consume) will keep the savings rate at about 10 per cent during the projection period. Consumers' expenditure is thus likely to continue to grow throughout the projection period. In line with official projections, government consumption is also projected to rise up to mid-1984 despite some further reduction in employment. Public sector investment is expected to be strongly expansionary in 1983/84 but by mid-1984 it may still be about 63 per cent below the level of the ten years earlier. The reversal of the downward trend in public sector investment reflects official encouragement to all parts of the public sector to raise investment[59], the assumption being that part of the fiscal adjustment in order to raise the PSBR to its original planed level of 2¾ per cent of GDP in 1983/84 will take the form of higher capital spending.

After declining a little up to mid-1983, private non-residential investment is expected to rise moderately from mid-1983 onwards. Profits, though remaining weak by past standards, are expected to recover a little further. The significant restructuring in industry and services with the view to reducing labour costs and a small decline in real interest rates could also contribute to the rise in capital deepening investment. However, investment in manufacturing is likely to be weak reflecting the substantial margin of unutilised capacity, sluggish world demand at least up to mid-1983 and the weak cost and price competitiveness of wide sectors of British industry and services[60]. The projections imply continuing disinvestment and hence a further decline in net capital stock in manufacturing. On the contrary, investment in distribution and services is projected to continue rising moderately during the projection period.

For the same reasons which led to the upturn in the second half of 1981 (improved earnings/house price ratio, availability of finance and falling mortgage rates), private residential investment should rise strongly up to mid-1984. It is also assumed that some inventory accumulation will start in mid-1983, imparting a positive contribution to real GDP growth up to mid-1984. However, stock/output ratios are expected to remain at historically low levels. Technological changes, the tendency of producers and traders to hold lower stocks than in the past, the weak profit outlook and high real interest rates mitigate against a significant build-up of stocks.

Continuous growth of total domestic demand averaging 2 per cent (annual rate) over the three half-years to mid-1984 is expected to be partly offset by the deterioration in the real foreign balance giving an annual rate of growth of real GDP of 1¾ per cent during the projection period. The growth of manufacturing output will be somewhat less, reflecting the continuous loss of external and domestic market shares. The actual growth of real GDP is relatively weak for a recovery phase. As there is still over-manning in industry and as a sizeable part of the sustained expansion of investment in services in recent years has been labour saving, employment is likely to decline continuously up to mid-1984 with overall productivity growth at about 3¼ per cent in 1983 before falling to a little less than 2 per cent in the first half of 1984. In manufacturing, productivity growth is expected to come down gradually to about 2¾ per cent, annual rate, in the first half of 1984. On this basis, the decline in total

59. Local authorities in particular have been urged not to underspend on capital projects as they have been in the recent period.

60. Despite the projected recovery, private non-residential investment in the first half of 1984 would be below the level of two years earlier, and manufacturing investment (including leasing) below the 1965 level. Manufacturing investment is expected to fall by 4 per cent in 1983 and about 2 per cent, annual rate, in the first half of 1984.

employment would slow down from 2¼ per cent in 1982 to some ¼ per cent in the first half of 1984 with unemployment (including school leavers) reaching 13¼ per cent[61] of the total labour force by mid-1984.

The unusually large deterioration of external competitiveness over the last few years will continue to affect trade flows in a way that econometric relationships based on past trends may fail to capture. In the past, both export prices and profits on exportables (and on import-competing goods) moved relatively smoothly whereas since 1979 the former experienced an extraordinarily big rise and the latter an equally important decline, with many companies actually incurring heavy losses. Under these conditions, a sizeable deterioration in competitiveness has two important effects :

   i) In view of the relative price rise of British goods, importers shift to other producers and British consumers switch to imports.

   ii) Supply is affected as the loss of profits on exports and weak domestic demand lead over time to a reduction in output and capacity.

The second effect is assumed to become more important over the projection period. However, this will be largely offset by the recent (in the two months to January 1983) sharp decline in the effective exchange rate and the ensuing marked improvement in competitiveness, whose effects will gain strength early in 1984 thus limiting the loss in export market shares to probably less than 1 per cent, which is significantly below the long-run trend loss of the past twenty-two years.

After two years of decline, the volume of non-oil merchandise exports is projected to rise in 1983 and in the first half of 1984. This, coupled with continuing important rises in oil exports and a recovery in service exports will result in a growth of total exports of goods and services of about 3½ per cent, annual rate, in the eighteen months to mid-1984. Import penetration, however, is forecast to continue at a sustained pace with non-oil imports (volume) increasing at some 5 per cent annual rate during 1983 and the first half of 1984. But with slowly growing service imports and declining oil imports, the volume increase in total imports of goods and services is projected to be 4¼ per cent (annual rate). The implied import elasticity (non-oil) with respect to total demand[62] is about 2¼ on average in the three half-years to mid-1984. The ensuing deterioration in the real foreign balance combined with broadly unchanged terms of trade will turn around the trade account from surplus in 1982 to near balance in 1984. However, in view of the large invisible surplus, the current account is projected to remain in moderate surplus during the projection period.

## IV.  MANUFACTURING INDUSTRY AND STRUCTURAL ADJUSTMENT

The main changes in the industrial structure of the economy since 1960 summarised in Diagram 10 are characterised by the continuing rise in the share of services sector in total GDP, the increasing share of energy since 1976 and the accelerating decline in the share of manufacturing industry after the second oil price shock and coinciding with loss of competitiveness and tight macro-economic policies. The most marked change has been the relative decline in manufacturing industry from

---

61.  Unemployment is based on the old definition which includes job seekers not entitled to receive unemployment benefits. The unemployment rate on the basis of the new definitions will be 12½ per cent.
    62.  Including exports.

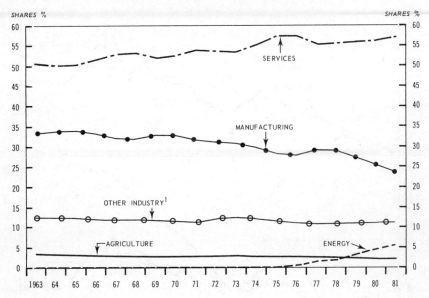

*Diagram 11.* **Industrial composition of output**

1. Excluding oil.

*Sources: National Income and Expenditure,* CSO, 1982 edition.

about 31 per cent of GDP[63] in the four years to 1974 to less than 25 per cent on average over the four years to 1981. Since 1978 manufacturing output has fallen absolutely and substantially more below trend than total output (Diagram 11). Though to varying degrees almost all OECD countries after 1974 experienced some change in the structure of output, none recorded as large a relative decline in manufacturing as the United Kingdom; and contrary to the United Kingdom, manufacturing output in all other OECD countries except Sweden continued to be on a rising trend after 1974.

With the Government's emphasis on supply-side policies and the priority given to reducing the public sector's claims on resources so as to make room for private sector expansion, the ability of manufacturing industry to meet a rise in demand is of central importance to the medium-term policy approach. This Part of the Survey starts with an analysis of the performance of manufacturing industry since the first oil shock in 1973. The second section then examines briefly some aspects of the Government's micro-economic adjustment and industrial policies which need to be seen within the context of the macro-economic approach of giving priority to the reduction of inflation as a precondition for attaining sustained growth.

*Manufacturing industry*

For a long period, manufacturing industry was plagued by structural difficulties stemming from historically low investment ratios, management inefficiency, inadequate marketing policies and restrictive labour practices and labour disputes which hindered innovation and technological progress. However, the underlying weaknesses of manufacturing industry were not always fully evident up to the first oil crisis:

63. In current prices.

41

*Diagram 12.* **Output trends**

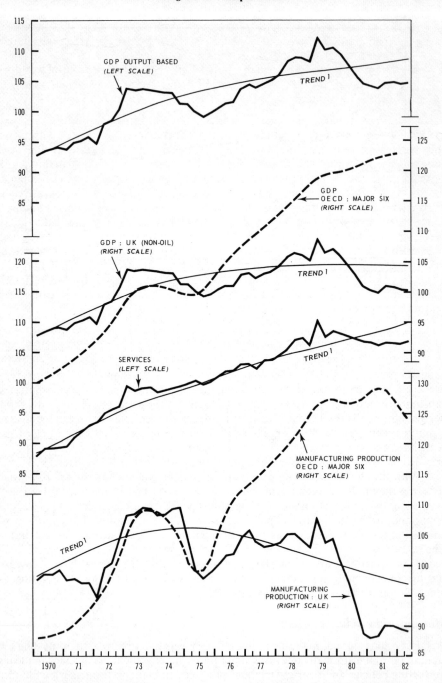

1. The trend values have been estimated using the Phase-Average Trend Method (PAT), U.K.
*Sources: National Income and Expenditure,* CSO and *National Accounts,* OECD.

*i)* During the period of rapid growth of world trade in the 1950s and 1960s, world markets were mainly dominated by sellers.

*ii)* The continuing special trading relationship with most Commonwealth countries and newly-independent countries provided a strong advantage to British exports up to the late 1960s.

*iii)* From the mid-1960s up to the early 1970s, the gradual build-up of world-wide inflationary pressures concealed the deterioration in the competitiveness of British manufacturing.

After 1974, rapidly changing world economic patterns, notably the turnaround from supply-dominated to demand-dominated world markets associated with increasingly aggressive price and non-price competition by the old industrial and newly-industrialised countries, contributed importantly to the weakening of manufacturing output. It also seems likely that non-price factors such as delivery times, design and quality worked increasingly against British goods in world markets. Comparatively low levels of research and development expenditure probably contributed also. Among the major industrialised countries, the United Kingdom occupied, in the second half of the 1970s, the second lowest place in the OECD area in total research and development expenditure as a per cent of manufacturing value added and total research and development per employee in the private manufacturing sector was half that of the major European industrialised countries. More recently, the marked loss of international competitiveness – discussed in Part I above – has been a major cause of the deterioration in the performance of manufacturing industry.

The de-industrialisation process after the first oil crisis has manifested itself in many different ways which are interconnected. After rising at an annual rate of about 3¼ per cent in the ten years to 1974, manufacturing investment has since on average

Table 12. **Investment performance in manufacturing**
Annual percentage rate of change

| | $\dfrac{1971}{1962}$ | $\dfrac{1980}{1971}$ | 1977 | 1978 | 1979 | 1980 | 1981 | 1982[1] |
|---|---|---|---|---|---|---|---|---|
| Total investment[2] | 3.3 | 0.4 | 6.0 | 10.6 | 7.3 | −6.4 | −13.5 | −7.1 |
| *of which:* | | | | | | | | |
| Investment in plant and machinery | 4.1 | 1.3 | 4.1 | 10.9 | 7.8 | −4.8 | −13.0 | −9.9 |
| Net capital stock in plant and machinery | | | | | | | | |
| Estimate A[2][3] | 4.4 | 2.4 | 1.9 | 2.3 | 2.3 | 1.2 | −0.5 | −1.2 |
| Estimate B[2][3] | 4.4 | 1.7 | 0.8 | 1.1 | 1.0 | −0.3 | −2.3 | −4.0 |
| Capital labour ratio A | 4.8 | 4.5 | 1.6 | 2.8 | 3.7 | 7.5 | 10.5 | 4.7 |
| Capital labour ratio B | 4.8 | 3.7 | 0.5 | 1.6 | 2.1 | 5.8 | 8.2 | 2.0 |
| Productivity of capital | | | | | | | | |
| Estimate A[2][3] | −1.2 | −2.6 | — | −1.7 | −2.1 | −10.1 | −5.8 | 1.3 |
| Estimate B[2][3] | −1.2 | −1.9 | 1.1 | −0.5 | −0.8 | −8.8 | −4.1 | 4.3 |
| Relative Labour/Capital cost[4] | 3.7 | 2.7 | −4.8 | 1.9 | 5.5 | 4.9 | 6.8 | 6.5 |

1. The 1982 figures are Secretariat estimates.
2. Including leased assets.
3. The subscripts A and B represent Secretariat estimations of net capital stock assuming reduced life time for equipment. In the case A the average life time was reduced from 19 years in 1973 to 13 years in 1982. In the case B the respective reduction was from 19 years in 1973 to 9 years in 1982.
4. Compensation per employee relative to the price of capital (deflator of equipment).
*Sources: National Income and Expenditure,* CSO 1982; direct communication from CSO and OECD Secretariat estimates.

declined somewhat[64]. Investment in plant and machinery, which is more important from the point of view of the longer-run potential output growth than investment either in new buildings or in transport equipment, has traditionally been the strongest component. And though again it held up much better over the last ten years than total investment, it still experienced a marked deceleration in its trend rate of growth from about 4 per cent in the ten years to 1974 to slightly less than 1 per cent since then. After allowing for the accelerated obsolescence and scrapping rates (following the marked rise in energy prices and the accompanying shifts in production technologies), net investment in plant and machinery swung even more, turning negative after 1980[65] (Table 12).

Accordingly, after rising at a sustained rate of about 4½ per cent up to 1970, the growth of net capital stock in plant and machinery steadily decelerated during the 1970s before turning negative in 1980. Over the three years to 1982 it has been estimated by the Secretariat that net capital stock may have declined by up to about 7 per cent, thus underlying the shrinkage in the manufacturing sector. These figures probably underestimate somewhat the reduction in productive capacity in manufacturing because in the face of steeply rising labour costs, investment may have become more capital intensive. Similarly, after the first oil crisis, energy saving investment as in other OECD countries, has further raised the capital/output ratio. Accordingly, the combined impact of the falling net capital stock and higher capital/output ratio of new investment has had a marked effect on capacity in manufacturing over the last few years.

Another factor which had a significant negative effect on the potential growth of manufacturing after 1975 is the marked decline in labour productivity growth which is, of course, associated with the disappointing net investment trend already noted. In fact, productivity growth fell from a long-run trend rate of 3¾ per cent, annual rate, up

Table 13. **Labour costs in manufacturing**
Average annual percentage change

| | 1973 1962 | 1981 1973 | 1974 | 1975 | 1976 | 1977 | 1978 | 1979 | 1980 | 1981 |
|---|---|---|---|---|---|---|---|---|---|---|
| Compensation per employee | 8.8 | 17.6 | 22.3 | 29.4 | 18.5 | 10.4 | 13.1 | 15.6 | 18.5 | 13.9 |
| Real compensation per employee[1] | 3.4 | 2.3 | 4.3 | 4.6 | 2.5 | −4.1 | 3.9 | 2.5 | 2.1 | 2.7 |
| Real labour costs per employee[2] | 4.3 | 2.2 | 7.7 | 0.4 | 3.6 | −6.3 | 0.1 | 7.7 | −1.3 | 6.6 |
| Productivity | 4.2 | 0.6 | −1.5 | −2.6 | 5.3 | 1.6 | 1.1 | 1.3 | −3.7 | 3.9 |
| Real wage gap[3] | 0.1 | 1.5 | 9.2 | 3.0 | −1.7 | −7.9 | −1.0 | 6.7 | 2.5 | 2.9 |
| Unit labour costs | 4.4 | 16.8 | 24.1 | 32.9 | 12.5 | 8.7 | 11.8 | 14.0 | 22.5 | 8.8 |
| *Memorandum items:* | | | | | | | | | | |
| Employment in manufacturing | −0.6 | −3.1 | 0.2 | −4.5 | −3.1 | 0.3 | −0.5 | −1.1 | −5.8 | −9.8 |
| Share of labour compensation in total value added in manufacturing[4] | 71.5 | 78.7 | 78.7 | 81.1 | 79.8 | 74.2 | 73.7 | 78.9 | 80.7 | 82.8 |

1. Compensation per employee deflated by the private consumption deflator.
2. Compensation per employee deflated by the manufacturing production implicit price deflator.
3. Real labour cost growth minus productivity growth, adjusted for terms of trade effects.
4. Including national insurance surcharge.
*Sources: National Income and Expenditure 1982, CSO; Secretariat estimates.*

64. The average level of investment at 1975 prices in the ten years to 1981 was about 5 per cent below that of the three years to 1971. The 1970 peak investment was only exceeded in 1979 before investment turned down again so that in 1982 it is estimated to fall to the same level as in 1965.
65. The United Kingdom National Accounts do not take into account the accelerated rate of obsolescence after 1973 in estimating net fixed investment. Accordingly, the Secretariat has made some tentative estimates taking into account this factor. These are discussed in detail in Annex I.

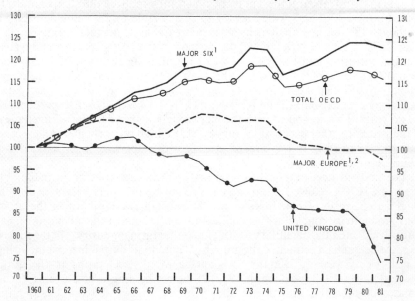

*Diagram 13.* **International comparisons in employment in industry**

1. Excluding United Kingdom.
2. Germany, France, Italy, Belgium, Netherlands, Sweden.
*Source: Labour Statistics,* OECD.

to the first oil shock in 1973/74 to barely above ½ per cent up to 1980. Even allowing for the productivity upsurge in the two years to 1982, the longer-run trend rate since 1973/74 was about 1½ per cent, or less than half that in the previous decade. In addition to cyclical factors, notably weak demand over a number of years, which depressed productivity growth after 1973/74, the slower growth of net capital stock had also a significant adverse impact. Secretariat estimates indicate that the deceleration in the trend rate of increase in the ratio of net capital stock in plant and machinery to employment (from around 5 per cent in the 1960s to 4 per cent in the late 1970s) may explain about one-fifth of the slowdown in the growth of labour productivity since 1973/74. Cyclical and other structural factors account for most of the other four-fifths. The deceleration in this ratio and the related slowdown in productivity growth, by reducing the pace of technological expansion in industry, could become an important impediment to sustained growth in manufacturing over the medium-run.

Though the fall in manufacturing employment since the early 1970s is the direct consequence of the declining output trend, in a long-run context falling employment in turn negatively affects the growth of "potential" output. The decline in manufacturing employment started in 1971, originally for cyclical reasons but with the structural causes becoming more important over time, especially after 1979. The rise in the cost of labour relative to that of capital by stimulating substitution of capital for labour played a role but less so than the cyclical factors. Manufacturing employment declined at a trend-rate of just over 2 per cent in the ten years to 1980 with the decline gathering momentum to 8 per cent, annual rate, over the two years to 1982. As a result, the cumulative fall reached 31 per cent in the twelve years to 1982 and the share of manufacturing employment in total dependent employment fell to around 27 per cent in 1982 compared with 36½ per cent in 1970 and 39 per cent in 1960.

The appreciable decline in employment not only led to an important contraction of the total industrial labour force, but more importantly reduced the number of the highly qualified professional and skilled labour force available to the manufacturing sector. And though the fall in employment of the more qualified manufacturing labour force appears to have been relatively small during most of the 1970s, more recently, given the prolonged recession and the higher cost of maintaining this type of labour force, it appears that the rate of lay-offs was higher than for the unskilled. Indeed, the proportion of unemployed skilled labour in total unemployment, after remaining broadly stable at about 10 per cent between the mid-1970s and 1980, rose to just over 15 per cent over the last two years. This combined with the increasingly longer duration of unemployment and the switch to other occupations suggest that a high proportion of skilled personnel has been permanently lost to manufacturing with important repercussions over the medium-term[66].

The marked deceleration in the growth of net capital stock in manufacturing during the 1970s followed by an actual decline in the more recent period, higher capital/output ratio of new investment, the substantial slowdown in the growth of labour productivity coupled with a continuous contraction of the labour force, have all negatively affected the potential growth of manufacturing industry. On the basis of the above, the Secretariat estimated the growth of "potential" output in manufacturing over the last twenty years[67]. Diagram 14 shows a rapid deceleration in the growth of "potential" after 1973, peaking in 1977/78 before turning negative since then. Two estimates of potential growth are shown based on two different assumptions on scrapping rates after the first oil shock. Both estimates show an acceleration in the rate of decline of "potential" over the last two years, with the one incorporating the faster scrapping rate showing a level of potential output in 1982 at about 6 per cent below the one with the slower scrapping rate. Despite the fall in potential, there is an important margin of unused capacity reflecting the marked decline in demand. Assuming that the potential level of manufacturing output lay between the two limits included above, the margin of unutilised capacity can be estimated at about 15 per cent in 1982, which is a post-war peak.

Business surveys bear out the findings on unused capacity. In 1976, 25 per cent of firms reported working at full capacity and though output had fallen by 7 per cent in 1980, 25 per cent continued to report working at full capacity suggesting a fall in capacity over this period. Superimposing the replies of the business surveys on the "gap" (between potential and actual output based on Secretariat studies), Diagram 14 shows that both move together and the gap tracks the turning point very well. On the basis of past relationships, the curve representing the business replies should have been considerably below the estimated level of gap in 1981 and 1982 which suggests that either the potential output has fallen considerably faster than estimated by the Secretariat and/or that businessmen, after so many years working below capacity, have lowered their norms of what they consider full capacity. However, whichever measure is used and whichever assumption regarding obsolescence and scrapping rate is applied, it shows clearly that the margin of unutilised capacity in 1982 remains substantial.

The estimates above and detailed in Annex I suggest two main conclusions. The first is that there has been an absolute decline in manufacturing capacity which has given rise to a major imbalance between physical capacity and the labour force. The latter has occurred in other Member countries but generally manufacturing capacity has continued to expand – although at a slower rate than earlier – so that the situation is particularly severe in the United Kingdom. The second conclusion is that despite the fall

---

66. A small proportion of skilled labour on the unemployment registers is due to the ongoing technological change which makes certain skills redundant.

Diagram 14. **Potential output in manufacturing**

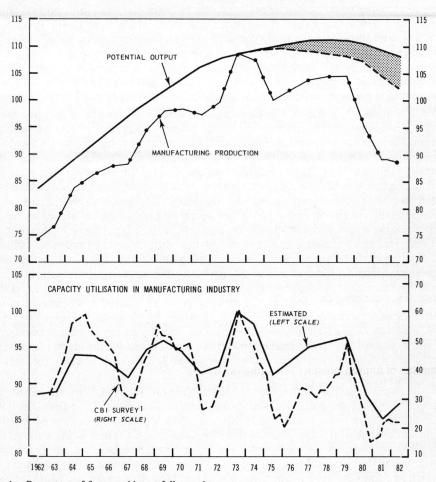

1. Percentage of firms working at full capacity.
*Source:* OECD Secretariat estimates.

in capacity there is still an important margin of slack, indicating that the capacity available to meet a pick-up in demand is sizeable. It seems that a stumbling block in utilising the capacity lies with the ability of British industry to compete for orders against foreign suppliers. This is borne out by the October 1982 CBI Survey of Industrial Trends which indicated further declines in orders and output despite the recovery in consumer demand.

*Positive adjustment and industrial policies*

OECD Ministers in June 1978 agreed on general orientations for policies to facilitate structural adjustments needed to sustain faster economic growth. It was agreed that a shift towards more positive adjustment policies was required so as to permit as far as possible the encouragement by market forces of the gradual movement of capital and labour to their most productive uses. At their meeting in May 1982,

OECD Ministers reiterated the need for structural adjustment to cope with the impediments to better economic performance. In particular, they stressed that policies "to permit structural change at the maximum speed which is politically feasible and socially acceptable, would greatly contribute to establishing the pre-conditions for increased economic growth, high employment, lower inflation and improved international trade relations". This section examines briefly some aspects of the Government's micro-economic adjustment and industrial policies which need to be seen within the context of the macro-economic approach described in Part II above.

The main objectives of the Government's micro-policies are to improve market efficiency and industrial performance so that private enterprise can take advantage of profitable investment opportunities. Central to these aims is the removal of barriers to the operation of market forces. In 1979, exchange controls were abolished as were those on pay, prices and dividends. Regulations concerning office development have been abolished and those covering industrial development suspended. The administration of land use controls has been made more efficient. More recently, restrictions on hire purchase and instalment credit were lifted. Fiscal measures have been taken with a view to increasing incentives and fostering enterprises and initiative; these include reductions in marginal rates of taxation, the easing of the corporation tax burden on industrial companies by making more generous industrial building allowances and changes in the stock relief scheme, removal of tax disincentives to mergers and improvements in capital taxation (increased reliefs, lower rates and wider rollover provisions). As an experiment to see whether industrial and commercial activity can be fostered by the removal of some fiscal imposts[68] and a marked reduction in statutory regulations, the Government since 1979 has established eleven "enterprise zones" mainly in the more depressed areas. These zones ranging from about 60 to 400 hectares will receive the above incentives for ten years. A further 13 zones have been announced. It is too early to assess the impact of the enterprise zones.

As an integral part of the programme to regenerate industrial growth, considerable incentives have been granted to small and medium-sized firms. To increase the flow of capital to these firms the Business Start-up Scheme – introduced in May 1981 – provides an outside investor in a new firm[69] with income tax reliefs on investments up to £10 000 per year. In addition, under the Loan Guarantee Scheme, the Government makes available guarantees on 80 per cent of each loan by participating banks to a firm which has difficulty in financing a worthwhile project. Also, under the Venture Capital Scheme, losses in equity investments in unquoted trading companies by investment companies and individuals can be set against income tax liability. Small companies also benefit from a reduction in their tax rate and other measures such as the Small Workshop Scheme which grants considerable tax privileges[70]. The amount of official control, administrative and other bureaucratic burdens on small firms have been reduced.

Other important aspects of adjustment and industrial policies concern regional assistance and nationalised industries and publicly-owned companies.

    *i)* The main expenditures in the past and planned up to 1984/85 on regional policies by the three Government Departments concerned are shown in

---

67.  See Annex I for details.

68.  The zones are exempt from rates and development land tax, receive 100 per cent capital allowances for industrial and commercial buidings, have absence in most cases from planning controls and Industrial Development Certificates and benefit from streamlining of some customs and warehousing procedures.

69.  Established within the last five years.

70.  Under this Scheme, a 100 per cent allowance against corporation tax is granted on the construction of industrial buildings of 2 500 square feet or less.

Table 14. **Industrial and regional support expenditures**[1]

£m, current prices

| | 1976-1977 | 1977-1978 | 1978-1979 | 1979-1980 | 1980-1981 | 1981-1982 | 1982-1983 | 1983-1984 | 1984-1985 |
|---|---|---|---|---|---|---|---|---|---|
| **Department of Industry** | | | | | | | | | |
| Regional and general industrial support | 519 | 502 | 629 | 509 | 644 | 807 | 534 | 680 | 590 |
| Scientific and technological assistance | 98 | 100 | 106 | 142 | 344 | 212 | 249 | 280 | 300 |
| Support for aerospace, shipbuilding, steel and vehicle manufacture | 351 | 349 | 326 | 376 | 599 | 1 043 | 606 | 60 | — |
| Other central and miscellaneous services | 25 | 29 | 32 | 35 | 42 | 48 | 51 | 50 | 50 |
| | 993 | 980 | 1 094 | 1 062 | 1 628 | 2 109 | 1 440 | 1 070 | 940 |
| **Department of Energy** | | | | | | | | | |
| Regional and general industrial support | 9 | 20 | 16 | 22 | 29 | 27 | 32 | 30 | 20 |
| Scientific and technological assistance | 148 | 127 | 143 | 174 | 218 | 264 | 265 | 270 | 280 |
| Support for nationalised industries | 82 | 100 | 193 | 266 | 265 | 398 | 778 | 200 | 230 |
| Other central and miscellaneous services | 15 | 32 | 31 | -16 | 14 | 25 | 26 | 30 | 30 |
| | 253 | 279 | 385 | 445 | 526 | 715 | 1 101 | 530 | 560 |
| **Department of Trade** | | | | | | | | | |
| Regional and general industrial support | 15 | 15 | 18 | 23 | 26 | 29 | 33 | 30 | 30 |
| Export Credit Guarantee Department | 725 | -146 | 359 | -50 | -155 | 85 | 367 | 190 | 310 |
| Total outlays | 1 986 | 1 128 | 1 856 | 1 480 | 2 025 | 2 938 | 2 941 | 1 830 | 1 850 |

1. The table does not include expenditures on such items as export promotion (£20 million in 1981-1982), support for the Civil Aviation Authority and regulations of domestic trade and industry and consumer protection.
*Source:* *The Government's Expenditure Plans 1982-1983 to 1984-1985*, Vol. 2, HMSO, Cmnd. 8494-11, 1982.

Table 14. The largest item is regional development grants (RDG) which after falling sharply in 1979/80 rose by 52 and 22 per cent in the following two years respectively. As Table 14 shows, there was a planned reduction in 1982/83 but, mainly because of the recent ending of the RDG deferment, expenditure for 1982-83 is likely to rise slightly above that for 1981-82. A reduction of 20 per cent between 1982/83 and 1983/84 is now planned. The main objective of regional policy is to foster new investment in the more depressed areas and particularly those most affected by declining industries. The coverage of assisted areas has been reduced from 44 to 27 per cent of the population, development grants have been cut for some areas and stricter criteria for selective grants introduced.

ii) Outlays on nationalised industries and publicly-owned companies have increased rapidly in recent years largely reflecting assistance for BL Ltd.[71], and the steel and coal industries. In 1982/83, support for BL Ltd. and the steel industry is planned to be substantially reduced while grants to the coal industry are expected to more than double to £598 million. The basic aim has been to finance necessary rationalisation including labour shedding and capital investment to enable these industries to become more efficient. At the same time a number of public enterprises have been sold wholly or in part to the private sector with the aim of improving their efficiency. Further privatisation is planned.

As can be seen from Table 14, expenditure on industrial and regional support after increasing sharply in 1981/82 is planned to be slightly lower in 1982/83 – implying a considerable fall in real terms – and then fall substantially in the two following years. The areas in which the reduced outlays will occur have not been announced by the Government but in part will reflect the planned lower level of support for BL Ltd. Some increase in expenditures is likely for research and development and the introduction of new technologies. The estimates in Table 14 do not include outlays on labour market programmes aimed at improving the quality of the labour force and efficiency of labour markets which are projected to cost £2 670 million in 1982/83[72] and which are discussed in Part I above and in Annex II. Expenditure on labour market measures are planned to rise slowly in nominal terms in the two years to 1984/85. Estimates of the fiscal costs of adjustment and industrial policies are not available but in view of the numerous measures taken since early 1979, in addition to ongoing costs of earlier programmes, they are likely to have risen somewhat.

This brief summary shows that the United Kingdom has taken a number of measures to foster more efficient industry which accord broadly with the OECD Ministers recommendations on positive adjustment. At the same time, however, the increase in outlays on industrial and regional support may to some extent have hindered structural change. Also, the competitive benefits granted to firms starting up in the enterprise zones may run counter to the positive adjustment recommendations. Moreover, the efficiency of the micro-adjustment policies have probably been hampered by the loss of competitiveness related to exchange rate developments stemming partly from the tight stance of macro-economic policy. In 1981/82 outlays by the Department of Industry were £550 million (36 per cent) higher than projected in March 1981. The votes for the Departments of Energy and Trade were exceeded by 49 and 30 per cent respectively to give a total overrun of 38 per cent (£850 million). A considerable part of this overrun is attributable to the vehicle, steel and coal industries which have been severely hit by the weakness of demand and import penetration. Also, because of the

71. Producers of Leyland vehicles.
72. Of which £1½ billion represents outlays on special employment programmes.

high real exchange rate whose effects do not discriminate between efficient and inefficient industries, the dynamic parts of industry which micro-policies are aimed to encourage are also affected. The difficulties of industry in competing with foreign suppliers is also increasing protectionist pressures which, unless eschewed, will add to inflationary pressures, distort resource allocation and reduce welfare.

# V.  CONCLUSIONS

Since 1979 the Government has given the highest priority to reducing inflation so as to provide the basis for the achievement of sustained non-inflationary growth over the medium term. The objectives continue to be sought through the pursuit of tight and steady demand-management policies which are non-accommodating to inflation – as described in the Medium Term Financial Strategy – and by steadily reducing the size of the PSBR to ensure ample resources for private setor expansion. At the same time, the Government has sought to strengthen the supply side of the economy through reducing the direct tax burden, privatisation of nationalised industries and the removal or reduction of institutional impediments to structural change. In the central area this policy approach has succeeded; in particular, the rate of inflation, influenced by weak import prices and later by lower pay settlements, has substantially fallen from a peak rate of over 20 per cent in the second half of 1979 to some 6 per cent in the year to December 1982, the lowest rate for over eleven years. The PSBR has been reduced relative to GDP and interest rates have come down markedly. Also, considerable progress has been made in the privatisation of public sector industries and deregulation through the removal of exchange controls, price and pay controls, hire purchase restrictions, and other measures.

The fall in output and employment has been severe and greater than initially envisaged by the authorities. This reflects the costs of adjustment to the Government's anti-inflationary and supply-side approach together with the effects of the world recession. However, the downturn in output and employment has been greater than in most other Member countries. While the onset of the world recession has contributed to the sharp fall in manufacturing production to a level some 16 per cent below the 1979 peak and the rise in unemployment from 5 per cent to 12 per cent of the workforce between mid-1979 and end-1982, domestic factors have been more important. The most significant has been the unprecedented loss of competitiveness stemming from the sharp rise in earnings in 1979 and 1980 and the appreciation of sterling. As shown in Part I above, international competitiveness measured in relative unit labour costs deteriorated by some 55 per cent between the average level in the five years to 1978 and 1981. Associated with this has been a sharp rise in real labour costs at a time of weak output and a marked squeeze on profits. Although there has been substantial improvement over the past eighteen months, the economy is still about 25 per cent less competitive than in the period up to 1978. Under these circumstances it is not surprising that the industrial base has contracted and unemployment risen strongly.

Against the background of a relatively weak world economy, the prospect over the next eighteen months is – on present policies and exchange rates – for a further small fall in the rate of inflation. Lower inflation and interest rates can be expected to stimulate real demand through its favourable effects on the volume of cash-controlled public expenditure, private sector real incomes and expenditure and private sector financial positions. But it is uncertain how strong these influences will be and whether they will be sufficient to provide the basis for a strong recovery. The Secretariat projections in Part IV above suggest that the recovery in demand will be weak. In particular, productive investment and exports – essential for sustaining growth – are not expected to recover to any extent. The projections also suggest that there will be further losses of export market shares accompanied by a deterioration of the current external account (including North Sea oil exports). On this basis, employment is projected to keep falling, though at a slower rate than in the recent period, and unemployment is likely to continue to rise up to mid-1984, the period covered in the projections.

The unsatisfactory outlook for the real economy might suggest that at first sight a considerable relaxation of policy would be appropriate. As shown in Part II above, fiscal policy has been tight for a considerable period and though its stance is now easier than it has been, it is still exerting a dampening effect. It is unlikely, however, that a marked recovery in output could be achieved – because of the large leakage to imports at present levels of competitiveness – through a marked easing of fiscal policy. While the growth of unit labour costs has been substantially reduced, the relative changes and projected movements against partner countries mean that improvements in competitiveness on account of slower wage rises will be difficult to achieve. There is perhaps more scope for further improvements in productivity, bringing United Kingdom average standards closer to those already achieved in some other OECD countries. Without better competitiveness, growth in the manufacturing sector is likely to remain depressed. It is sometimes suggested that another possibility of achieving a better competitive position is a lower exchange rate. There are obvious problems in looking for lasting improvement in competitiveness from this source. Inflation may rise because of higher import prices and their impact on pay settlements. Moreover, the Government has declared that it is opposed to such a course. Lower interest rates, even if exchange rates did not further adjust, would benefit competitiveness. While the recent falls in nominal interest rates are to be welcomed, real interest rates have stayed relatively high. Lower real rates would contribute to an improvement of the financial position of the non-oil, non-financial business sector and would be a necessary – though not a sufficient – condition for the recovery of private productive investment.

Even if any improvement in competitiveness is limited, there would nevertheless seem to be some scope for prudent relaxation of fiscal policy. Should the authorities, after taking account of the implication for interest rates, judge that a limited fiscal easing is appropriate, the type of stimulus is important. In view of the weak competitive position of the economy and the high level of import penetration, a reduction in personal income taxation would be unlikely to have worthwhile employment effects, the response of productive investment to increased consumers' expenditure is likely to be limited, and it would exacerbate the projected deterioration in the current external account. On the other hand, measures to reduce the personal taxation burden could be beneficial to incentives particularly at the lower end and to the climate for pay bargaining. In conditions of large imbalance between real wages and profits, an alternative approach would be fiscal measures to reduce industry's costs above those already announced in the Autumn Statement on 8th November, 1982. Compared with changes in personal income taxes, lower costs would be advantageous to profitability, improve the investment climate and help limit the contraction of capacity. The longer-term impact on employment could be expected to be larger. The outcome of both alternatives would be enhanced by higher public investment, and an increase in local authority capital spending was foreshadowed in the Autumn Statement.

Improved competitiveness coupled with prudent fiscal action would enable industry to take better advantage of the potential productivity gains which have developed from the sizeable reductions in overmanning, restrictive labour and business practices and other market rigidities over the last two years or so. Many of these changes are likely to be permanent and enable the economy to function more efficiently once it recovers. But an important question which remains is the extent to which the greater realism in private sector pay settlements and the trend towards plant-by-plant rather than centralised bargaining will be maintained when the labour market strengthens. The improvement in pay determination practices is encouraging and it is essential that it continues. This may well be facilitated – as emphasised by OECD Ministers in May 1982 – by strengthening the dialogue between the social partners. It would seem desirable that any further discussions between the social partners cover not only pay but the wider issues of the institutional rigidities in pay determination and the overall working and performance of the economy.

# CAPITAL STOCK, PRODUCTIVITY, AND POTENTIAL OUTPUT IN MANUFACTURING

## 1. Capital stock

Poor productivity and investment performance since the first oil shock and accelerated scrapping rate of the capital stock have significantly affected the level and growth of capacity. The official estimates of capital stock (included in the United Kingdom National Accounts) assume a constant scrapping rate based on an assumed average life time for equipment of 19 years. However, after 1973, higher energy and labour costs should have made some equipment and some "productive techniques" inefficient with a consequent loss in economic capacity. Because of the great uncertainty regarding the life-time of the existing and new equipment in a period of rapidly changing technology (partly due to high energy and labour costs and increased foreign competition) two assumptions have been retained[1]. The life time of equipment is falling gradually from 19 years in 1973 to 13 years by 1982 in assumption A and to 9 years by 1982 in assumption B. Moreover, the estimates of the stock of equipment include leased assets, which the United Kingdom official statistics do not include because they classify investment by ownership. The results of these estimates are shown in Table 12.

## 2. Productivity

There is a complex relationship between output growth and labour productivity. Sustained output growth is among the most important factors influencing productivity growth. The relationship between productivity and output known as the "Verdoorn law" has been tested over the 1962 to 1982 period for the manufacturing sector. The results are as follows:

*For the period 1962/1972*

(1)     $PRODMN = -0.7 + 1.1 \quad IPMN$
            $(-2.1) \quad (15.4)$
        $R^2 : 0.96 \quad DW : 0.80 \quad SE : 0.02$

*For the period 1962/82*

(2)     $PRODMN = -1.1 + 1.2 \quad IPMN$
            $(-1.0) \quad (5.2)$
        $R^2 : 0.56 \quad DW : 0.1 \quad SE : 0.1$

(3)     $PRODMN = 1.4 + 0.67 \quad IPMN + 0.2 \quad DUM1$
            $(1.7) \quad (3.7) \qquad (5.5)$
        $R^2 : 0.82 \quad DW : 0.6 \quad SE : 0.07$

where   PRODMN:  Productivity in manufacturing (log. form)
       IPMN:  Manufacturing production (log. form)
       DUM1:  Dummy variable taking value of  0 during 1964/72
                                                  1 during 1973/82.

The relationship gives a good fit up to the early seventies but the results are less satisfactory when the period is extended up to 1982. The elasticity of productivity growth with respect to output growth falls considerably in a period of low capacity utilisation as experienced in the seventies suggesting that other factors than output became more important. Accordingly a new equation has been estimated taking into account some of these factors such as capital formation in relation to employment, cyclical fluctuations, technological progress, etc., which affected substantially productivity growth in the 1970s.

---

1. These assumptions are based on econometric work done in the Secretariat and are roughly comparable with experience in other countries.

(4)    PRODMN = 1.54 + 0.679 CAPLAB + 0.817 DEV + 1.58 DUM1
            (11.2)   (21.0)                (4.1)         (6.35)
            − 0.35 DUM2 − 0.3 DUM3
            (−6.3)          (−1.3)

$R^2 = 0.993$    DW : 1.998    SE : 0.011

CAPLAB :  Capital/labour ratio (on the basis of assumption B regarding the life time of equipment, log. form)
DEV :     Deviation of manufacturing production from trend (log. form)
DUM1 :    Dummy variable taking value of 0 during 1964/72
                                        1 during 1973/82
DUM2 :    DUM1 multiplied by CAPLAB
DUM3 :    DUM1 multiplied by DEV.

The high significance of the coefficient of DUM2 shows that the impact of capital intensity in the second period was weaker, possibly influenced by a slowdown in embodied technological progress and innovation, a higher than assumed capital scrapping, energy substitution and changing management and manning practices.

## 3. Potential output

As there is no official estimate of potential output in manufacturing, a rough estimate of potential output growth has been obtained on the basis of the growth rate of labour input and long-run productivity. The labour force growth rate (adjusted for changes in hours worked and the falling share of manufacturing employment in total employment) has been used as a proxy of labour input growth, whereas long run labour productivity growth has been estimated as a function of the capital-labour ratio (using the coefficients estimated in equation No. 4). Finally, on the assumption that in 1973 the manufacturing sector was near full capacity, the level of manufacturing production in that year was used as a benchmark for the estimation of potential output (see Diagram 14 of the Survey).

*Annex II*

# EMPLOYMENT SCHEMES

Over the last eight years a number of employment-creating and training schemes have been introduced with the aim of saving jobs, alleviating youth unemployment, providing opportunities for temporary work and promoting structural changes in labour supply (notably by correcting skill mismatches).

## A. Training Schemes

The scope and the number of training schemes has been greatly expanded during the last five years, their share in total number of people covered by all employment schemes growing from 15 per cent in 1978 to around 45 per cent in mid-1982. Training schemes, although they have a smaller effect on the unemployment register, are more important over the longer run because new techniques of production create needs for more sophisticated skills which are not in sufficient supply. In this context, a new and more comprehensive training programme was elaborated in the beginning of 1982 to be applied over the next three years at a cost of £4 billion. The essential elements of this programme are:

*i)* The introduction of a new Youth Training scheme.

*ii)* Technical training to be more accessible to those who have the necessary ability.

*iii)* Definition (by 1985) of standards of competence for all main craft, technical and professional skills to replace time-serving and age-restricted apprenticeships.

*iv)* Better preparation for working life in initial full-time education.

*v)* More opportunities for vocational courses and better co-ordination of training and vocational education.

*vi)* A £16 million fund for development of schemes in particular localities or sectors.

Other training schemes already existing or planned to be implemented are set out below.

*Youth Opportunities Programme (YOP)*

This programme, first introduced in July 1977, provides a range of opportunities for unemployed young people (aged 16 to 17 years) for training courses and work experience schemes. Its aims are to prepare young people for work through employment induction courses, short training courses and work introduction courses, as well as work experience schemes on employers' premises, training workshops, community service and other special projects.

*Youth Training Scheme*

This scheme, which incorporates the main features of YOP, will become effective in September 1983 (replacing the YOP) and will offer twelve months training to some 460 000 unemployed school leavers (mostly 16 year-old), either in specialised colleges and/or in workplaces at an annual cost of £1 billion.

*Training in Industry*

This scheme provides funds to help where a shortfall in an industry's long-term training requirement is identified. Grants are made available to employers taking on apprentices and other long-term trainees additional to their normal requirement. This scheme will be subsumed under the Youth Training Scheme from September 1983.

*Training Opportunities Scheme*

This scheme provides training courses for adults mainly in skill centres and colleges. In 1980/81 over 60 000 trainees completed these courses.

## B. Employment Saving and Employment-Creating Schemes

*The Temporary Short-time Working Compensation Scheme*

This scheme was introduced on 1st April, 1979, as a replacement for the Temporary Employment Subsidy Scheme and was initially planned to remain open for applications until 31st March, 1980. (It is actually winding down rapidly as the number of people covered by the scheme has been falling rapidly from around one million in the first quarter of 1981 to some 123 000 in mid-1982). Its main purpose is to defer redundancies by adopting short-time working. Compensation is paid at the rate of 50 per cent of normal earnings for a maximum period of nine months (for new applicants since July 1982 the period is reduced to six months).

*Job Release Scheme*

This scheme which was introduced on 3rd January, 1977, enables employees approaching retirement age to retire earlier in return for a weekly allowance, on condition that the replacement must be recruited from the unemployment register (though not necessarily in exactly the same job). Three schemes are at present in operation.

   *i)* For all men aged 64 or more and women aged 59 or more.
   *ii)* For disabled men aged 60 or more.
   *iii)* For all men aged 63 or more (started in November 1981), and for all men aged 62 or more (from February 1982).

Weekly tax-free allowances are £55 for a married person with a dependent spouse and £43 for a single person. Closing date for applications is March 1984. The number of people covered in mid-1982 was 70 000.

*Community Industry*

Provides jobs for personally and socially disadvantaged young people who undertake work projects of benefit to the community. The scheme is financed through a grant to the National Association of Youth Clubs and covers about 7 000 adult and young workers.

*Community Enterprise Programme*

Replacing the Special Temporary Employment Programme, this programme provides temporary employment for long-term unemployed adults on projects of benefit to the community. It is restricted to people aged 18 to 24 years who have been unemployed for over six months and those aged 25 years and over who have been unemployed for over twelve months (priority is given to high unemployment areas). The scheme covers 30 000 young workers.

*Community Programme Scheme*

As from 1st October, 1982, this programme brings together the Community Enterprise Programme and Community Industry and is expected to provide some 130 000 places (mostly part-time) of yearly duration, and it will be run on the same criteria as Community Enterprise Programme. The scheme is for two years and is expected to cost over £575 million a year (including the provision for 30 000 CEP places). However, if the saving in unemployment benefits is taken into account the net additional expenditure for the 100 000 places is estimated at £185 million.

*Young Workers Scheme*

This scheme came into operation on 4th January, 1982, and is designed to encourage employers to take on more young people at realistic wage rates. Under the scheme, employers can receive payments of £15 in respect of young people earning less than £40 a week, or £7.50 for those earning between £40 and £45 who are under 18, in the first year of employment. Payments are made for a maximum one year and the scheme is expected to cover in 1982 about 130 000 young people at a cost of £60 million.

*Job Splitting Scheme*

Under this scheme, a grant of £750 (to cover extra costs of training, etc.) will be paid during the first year to employers where the splitting of a job results in the recruitment of an unemployed person already claiming unemployment benefit, or it can be paid to avoid someone becoming redundant. The split job could be filled by:

   − two unemployed already receiving unemployment benefits;
   − two existing full-time employees (if at least one would have been made redundant);

- one unemployed and one full-time employee;
- two existing full-time employees becoming part-time if the employer recruits one or more unemployed.

This scheme will run from 3rd January, 1983, to 30th March, 1984.

*Enterprise Allowance*

This scheme (although experimental) aims at helping unemployed people who want to start up in business but who may be deterred by the fact that they would lose their entitlement to unemployment or supplementary benefit. A flat rate taxable allowance of £40 per week will be paid fortnightly for the first year of operation to people aged between 18 and 65 who live and set up business in the same area. At the time of application, they must have been unemployed for at least thirteen weeks and must be in receipt of unemployment or supplementary benefit. In addition, they must show that they have at least £1 000 to invest in their business.

**Special employment and training schemes**
Thousands, mid-year

|  | 1979 | 1980 | 1981 | 1982 |
|---|---|---|---|---|
| Temporary short-time working compensation scheme | 31.4 | 126.9 | 557.3 | 117 |
| Special temporary employment programme | 15.0 | 10.0 | – | – |
| Short-time working compensation scheme | 8.0 | – | – | – |
| Temporary employment subsidy | 62.4 | – | – | – |
| Job release scheme | 31.7 | 66.0 | 53.9 | 68 |
| Small firms employment subsidy | 41.9 | 17.7 | – | – |
| Youth opportunities programme | 70.0 | 85.0 | 160.0 | 205 |
| Adult employment subsidy | 1.1 | – | – | – |
| Community enterprise programme |  |  | 15.6 | 30 |
| Community industry | 5.4 | 6.2 | 6.7 | 7 |
| Young workers scheme |  |  |  | 71 |
| Job introduction scheme | 0.2 | – | – | – |
| Enterprise allowance |  |  | – | 0.7 |
| Training for skills | 25.7 | 12.6 | 29.3 | 35 |
| Total number of people covered | 293 | 324 | 823 | 534 |
| Register effect[1] | 180 | 190 | 305 | 300 |

1. Differences between the gross numbers of people supported by special measures and the net direct effect on registered unemployment arise mainly from three factors:
- deadweight: the extent to which individuals or companies are paid to do what they would have done anyway;
- substitution: subsidising the employment of one person at the expense of another;
- displacement: subsidising one firm at the cost of output or employment in another.
*Sources:* Department of Employment press notice and direct communication to the OECD.

# CALENDAR OF MAIN ECONOMIC EVENTS

## 1981

*4th June*

Announcement of extended tax reliefs for business start-up scheme.

*2nd July*

Announcement of increases in duties on tobacco, betting and gaming in order to make up the revenue loss from halving the 20 pence increase in derv duty initially proposed in the Budget.

*27th July*

Youth opportunities programme expanded.

*20th August*

New monetary control arrangements came into effect. The principal changes are:

i) The publication of Minimum Lending Rate is discontinued.
ii) Short-term interest rates to be kept within undisclosed band through open market operations.
iii) The requirement of banks to monitor a minimum reserve asset rate is abolished.
iv) The requirement of the London clearing banks to hold 1½ per cent of their eligible liabilities with the Bank in non-interest bearing form was abolished.
v) All banks and licenced deposit takers to hold ½ per cent of their eligible liabilities with the Bank.

*7th September*

The index-linked National Saving Certificates became available to all, regardless of age.

*1st October*

Clearing banks raised their basic lending rates from 14 to 16 per cent.

*8th October*

Building societies raised basic mortgage rate by 2 percentage points to 15 per cent.

*23th November*

Introduction of the Industrial Relations legislation, the main elements being:

– limitation of trade union immunities
– definition of trade disputes to be narrowed
– compensation for victims of closed-shop agreements.

*2nd December*

The Government announced several measures bearing on public expenditure in 1982/83 and on the pattern of National Insurance contributions. The main measures announced were:

– planning and control of public expenditure from 1982-83 financial year will be made in cash. Cash factors applicable to the public sector have been fixed to 4 per cent for pay and 9 per cent for price increases.
– employees contributions to National Insurance increased by 1 percentage point to 8.75 per cent of relevant earnings starting in April 1982.
– the lower and upper earnings limit raised respectively to £29.5 per week and £220 per week.
– the Treasury supplement to National Insurance fund reduced from 14½ per cent to 13 per cent.
– the flat rate contribution of self-employed raised from £3.40 a week to £3.75 a week.
– the rate support grant reduced from 59.1 per cent to 56 per cent.

*3nd December*

Clearing banks cut base rates from 15 to 14½ per cent.

*14th December*

A 25 per cent grant on eligible costs to be provided to the steel industry for rationalisation and other projects.

*15th December*

Announcement of a new training scheme for unemployed youth providing to 16 year-old school-leavers a year-long training combining work experience and further education.

## 1982

*4th January*

Young workers scheme came into effect providing a subsidy to employers of young people earning less than £40 per week. The scheme is expected to cover 130 000 young workers in the first year of operation at a cost of £60 million.

*22nd January*

Clearing banks lowered base rates from 14½ to 14 per cent.

*15th February*

British Gas Corporation to raise gas prices by 22 per cent (12 per cent in April and 10 per cent in October).

*18th February*

Electricity prices to rise by 10 per cent.

*24th February*

Clearing banks lowered base rates from 14 to 13½ per cent and building societies reduced basic mortgage rate by ½ to 14½ per cent.

*9th March*

The Budget introduced to Parliament:
  *i)* Personal allowances and tax thresholds increased by up to 14 per cent.
  *ii)* Excise duties increased by a rate slightly lower than inflation.
  *iii)* Pension rates and other social security benefits will be increased by 11 per cent in November 1982 (9 per cent for expected inflation and 2 per cent to compensate pensioners for last year's shortfall).
  *iv)* Exemption limit for gifts to charities increased from £200 000 to £250 000 and stamp duty on transfers to charities has been removed. VAT reliefs introduced for charities concerned with disabled.
  *v)* Mobility allowance increased by 10.9 per cent and will be wholly exempted from income tax.
  *vi)* National Insurance surcharge reduced by 1 percentage point to 2½ (from August 1982). An extra reduction of ½ per cent will be made between August 1982 and April 1983.
  *vii)* The supplementary Petroleum Duty to be abolished by the end of 1982.
  *viii)* The rate of Petroleum Revenue Tax to be increased from 70 to 75 per cent from January 1983.
  *ix)* A new system for advance payment of petroleum revenue tax introduced at the rate of 20 per cent of gross revenues, less an oil allowance of 1 million tonnes per year.
  *x)* The threshold for capital transfer tax to be increased by £5 000 to £55 000 while the rate bands for lifetime and death transfers and capital gains taxes will be indexed as other income tax allowances.
  *xi)* The target ranges for monetary growth will apply both to the two measures of money supply as well as to PSL2 and was fixed at 8-12 per cent (annual rate) for 1982-83 and 7-11 per cent for 1983-84.
  *xii)* An industrial energy package was introduced. The main elements are:
    – electricty charges to be reduced for users accepting load reduction,
    – a relief on gas prices will be given for large users,
    – foundry coke prices to remain unchanged,
    – the conversion scheme for oil-fired boilers to coal to be extended to service industries and manufacturing.

xiii) A package of measures worth £240 million to help construction industries announced:
- the Home Improvement Grant to be extended from 75 per cent to 90 per cent of eligible costs. Supplementary grants will be provided for home insulation.
- the Derelict Land Grant to be extended from 50 to 80 per cent of the cost of reclamation.
- capital allowances at the rate of 75 per cent (for the first year) introduced for new housing to be used wholly for letting.
- the exemption and the various thresholds for stamp duty on house purchase will be raised by £5 000.

xiv) A series of new and extended schemes for industrial innovation announced. These include additional assistance in space technology and production engineering and assistance for small engineering firms.

*11th March*

Clearing banks base rate reduced from 13½ to 13 per cent and building societies reduced mortgage rate to 13½ per cent.

*5th April*

A new industry bill published providing an extra £1 billion in industrial aid. Maximum single allocation of aid increased from £5 million to £10 million.

*4th May*

The Manpower Services Commission announced the transformation of Youth Opportunity programme into a twelve-month training programme for youths of 16 to 17 years of age as from September 1983.

*8th June*

Clearing banks cut base lending rate from 13 to 12½ per cent.

Announcement of a £60 million package of new measures to help investment in advance technologies.

*2nd July*

A new income bond introduced providing a regular monthly income (minimum holding £5 000 and maximum £200 000).

*25th July*

Announcement of the abolition of all remaining hire purchase controls.

*27th July*

Announcement of eleven new enterprise zones (seven in England, two in Scotland and one each in Wales and Northern Ireland).

Two new government schemes to help unemployed announced:
- a job-splitting grant (from 1.1.83 to 31.3.84) to help employers to provide more part-time work to unemployed.
- a community programme scheme (from 1.10.82) enabling long-term unemployed to do community work and voluntary activities.

*31st August*

Clearing banks base rates fall during August by 1½ percentage point to 10½ per cent.

*1st September*

Mortgage rates fell by 1½ percentage point to 12 per cent.

*8th November*

Financial Statement of the Chancellor of the Exchequer. The main measures announced are the following:
i) National Insurance Surcharge will be reduced by 1 percentage point from April next (relieving industry by about £700 million in the next fiscal year). Moreover, a further reduction equivalent to ½ per cent of National Insurance Surcharge for 1982/83 will be retroactively provided to private employers by reducing their National Insurance payments in the first three months of 1983. Public sector employers will not benefit from this measure as the estimated £400 million relief will be recovered through lower expenditure.
ii) From April next, National Insurance contribution rates will be increased from 8.75 to 9 per cent for employees and from 10.2 to 10.45 per cent for employers.

61

*iii)* The lower earnings limit increased to £32.5 per week in line with the single rate retirement pension and the upper earnings limit to £235. There will be similar increases for the self-employed.

*iv)* Social Security benefits will not be fully revalorised in 1983/84.

*v)* Council rents will not be raised more than inflation.

*vi)* Industrial gas prices will remain unchanged until autumn next year.

*vii)* Total public sector borrowing requirement is put at £96 billion or £½ billion less than forecast in the last Budget.

## *13th November*

Building societies cut mortgage rate by 2 percentage points to 10 per cent.

Announcement of a freeze on average electricity prices next year.

## **1983**

## *12th January*

Clearing banks base rates increased from 10½per cent to 11 per cent.

*STATISTICAL ANNEX*

# Table A. Expenditure on GDP
£ million

| | GDP at factor cost* | Final expenditure at market prices** | Total domestic demand*** | Consumers' expenditure | Public current expenditure | Fixed investment | Change in stocks | Exports of goods and services | Imports of goods and services | Indirect taxes less subsidies |
|---|---|---|---|---|---|---|---|---|---|---|
| | 1 | 2 | 3 | 4 | 5 | 6 | 7 | 8 | 9 | 10 |
| **At current prices:** | | | | | | | | | | |
| 1978 | 146 079 | 210 921 | 163 195 | 98 867 | 32 984 | 29 743 | 1 601 | 47 726 | 45 546 | 19 296 |
| 1979 | 167 937 | 247 984 | 192 859 | 117 071 | 38 324 | 34 469 | 2 995 | 55 125 | 54 616 | 25 431 |
| 1980 | 194 538 | 284 025 | 220 867 | 135 738 | 48 424 | 39 411 | −2 706 | 63 158 | 57 913 | 31 574 |
| 1981 | 211 411 | 309 267 | 241 445 | 151 286 | 54 942 | 39 377 | −4 160 | 67 822 | 60 730 | 37 126 |
| **At 1975 prices...** | | | | | | | | | | |
| 1970 | 85 498 | 118 668 | 97 092 | 57 814 | 19 103 | 19 460 | 802 | 21 576 | 23 938 | 9 151 |
| 1971 | 87 672 | 122 427 | 99 418 | 59 724 | 19 673 | 19 743 | 278 | 23 048 | 25 187 | 9 496 |
| 1972 | 88 833 | 126 923 | 103 558 | 63 270 | 20 484 | 19 823 | −19 | 23 318 | 27 694 | 10 224 |
| 1973 | 95 654 | 137 494 | 111 463 | 66 332 | 21 453 | 21 195 | 2 483 | 26 031 | 30 941 | 10 899 |
| 1974 | 94 966 | 136 670 | 108 786 | 65 049 | 21 774 | 20 562 | 1 401 | 27 884 | 31 243 | 10 461 |
| 1975 | 94 339 | 133 771 | 106 574 | 64 652 | 22 950 | 20 408 | −1 436 | 27 197 | 29 011 | 10 421 |
| 1976 | 97 793 | 138 778 | 109 183 | 64 707 | 23 178 | 20 640 | 658 | 29 595 | 30 234 | 10 751 |
| 1977 | 99 190 | 140 497 | 108 989 | 64 517 | 22 951 | 20 139 | 1 382 | 31 508 | 30 562 | 10 745 |
| 1978 | 102 284 | 145 748 | 113 656 | 68 227 | 23 438 | 20 845 | 1 146 | 32 092 | 31 754 | 11 710 |
| 1979 | 103 711 | 151 200 | 118 286 | 71 599 | 23 866 | 21 039 | 1 782 | 32 914 | 35 326 | 12 163 |
| 1980 | 101 488 | 147 806 | 114 749 | 71 550 | 24 311 | 20 443 | −1 555 | 33 057 | 34 143 | 12 175 |
| 1981 | 99 263 | 145 405 | 113 076 | 71 871 | 24 302 | 18 774 | −1 871 | 32 329 | 34 040 | 12 102 |
| **...and seasonally adjusted:** | | | | | | | | | | |
| 1981  1 | 25 160 | 35 993 | 28 143 | 18 040 | 6 055 | 4 690 | −642 | 7 850 | 7 673 | 3 160 |
| 2 | 24 790 | 35 975 | 27 947 | 17 926 | 6 048 | 4 667 | −694 | 8 028 | 8 249 | 2 936 |
| 3 | 24 446 | 36 629 | 28 498 | 17 934 | 6 127 | 4 663 | −226 | 8 131 | 9 240 | 2 943 |
| 4 | 24 867 | 36 808 | 28 488 | 17 971 | 6 072 | 4 754 | −309 | 8 320 | 8 878 | 3 063 |
| 1982  1 | 25 079 | 36 924 | 28 914 | 17 927 | 6 147 | 4 902 | −62 | 8 010 | 8 687 | 3 158 |
| 2 | 25 091 | 37 075 | 28 825 | 17 998 | 6 132 | 4 693 | 2 | 8 250 | 9 075 | 2 909 |
| 3 | 24 970 | 36 863 | 28 940 | 18 242 | 6 223 | 4 846 | −371 | 7 923 | 8 827 | 3 066 |

Note: For the years before 1973 the aggregates differ slightly from the sum of the components due to the method of rebasing to 1975 prices.

* 1 = 2 − 9 − 10.
** 2 = 4 + 5 + 6 + 7 + 8.
*** 3 = 2 − 8.
Source: Economic Trends.

Table B. Gross domestic fixed capital formation by sector and by type of asset and for selected industries
£ million at 1975 prices, seasonally adjusted

| | Total | Private sector[1] | General government[1] | Public corporations[1] | Vehicles, ships and aircraft | Plant and machinery | Dwellings Private | Dwellings Public | Other new building and works[2] | Petroleum and natural gas | Manufacturing[3] |
|---|---|---|---|---|---|---|---|---|---|---|---|
| 1969 | 18 954 | 10 390 | 5 385 | 3 201 | 1 694 | 6 043 | 2 187 | 2 087 | 7 352 | 97 | 3 877 |
| 1970 | 19 460 | 10 685 | 5 475 | 3 316 | 1 819 | 6 365 | 2 047 | 1 879 | 7 655 | 131 | 4 178 |
| 1971 | 19 743 | 11 099 | 5 297 | 3 334 | 1 882 | 6 264 | 2 440 | 1 733 | 7 781 | 139 | 3 896 |
| 1972 | 19 823 | 11 776 | 5 076 | 2 932 | 2 148 | 6 055 | 2 745 | 1 609 | 7 607 | 211 | 3 370 |
| 1973 | 21 195 | 12 267 | 5 793 | 3 135 | 2 416 | 6 775 | 2 449 | 1 703 | 7 852 | 327 | 3 440 |
| 1974 | 20 562 | 11 578 | 5 418 | 3 566 | 2 304 | 6 963 | 2 004 | 1 822 | 7 469 | 694 | 3 782 |
| 1975 | 20 408 | 11 504 | 4 984 | 3 920 | 2 041 | 6 658 | 2 182 | 1 967 | 7 560 | 1 374 | 3 522 |
| 1976 | 20 640 | 11 759 | 4 836 | 4 045 | 2 018 | 6 812 | 2 180 | 2 084 | 7 546 | 1 844 | 3 326 |
| 1977 | 20 139 | 12 419 | 4 018 | 3 702 | 2 182 | 6 969 | 2 039 | 1 874 | 7 075 | 1 698 | 3 476 |
| 1978 | 20 845 | 13 815 | 3 557 | 3 473 | 2 286 | 7 502 | 2 327 | 1 734 | 6 996 | 1 579 | 3 769 |
| 1979 | 21 039 | 14 186 | 3 414 | 3 439 | 2 421 | 8 253 | 2 017 | 1 598 | 6 750 | 1 295 | 3 969 |
| 1980 | 20 443 | 13 997 | 2 982 | 3 464 | 2 301 | 8 658 | 1 692 | 1 414 | 6 378 | 1 226 | 3 573 |
| 1981 | 18 774 | 13 460 | 2 147 | 3 167 | 1 883 | 8 361 | 1 430 | 916 | 6 184 | 1 356 | 2 938 |
| 1981  1 | 4 690 | 3 235 | 637 | 818 | 447 | 2 098 | 374 | 250 | 1 521 | 313 | 777 |
| 2 | 4 667 | 3 280 | 560 | 827 | 487 | 2 106 | 341 | 242 | 1 491 | 369 | 756 |
| 3 | 4 663 | 3 439 | 474 | 750 | 447 | 2 077 | 365 | 217 | 1 557 | 364 | 705 |
| 4 | 4 754 | 3 506 | 476 | 772 | 502 | 2 080 | 350 | 207 | 1 615 | 310 | 699 |
| 1982  1 | 4 902 | 3 608 | 482 | 818 | 504 | 2 086 | 377 | 258 | 1 661 | 361 | 696 |
| 2 | 4 693 | 3 498 | 373 | 831 | 453 | 2 051 | 379 | 231 | 1 625 | 366 | 660 |
| 3 | 4 846 | 3 588 | 458 | 819 | | | 391 | | | | 652 |

Note: Because individual components have not been revised they do not add up to the total.
1. Including purchases less sales of land and existing buildings.
2. Including transfer costs of land and buildings.
3. Excluding leased assets.
Source: Economic Trends.

## Table C. Consumption and investment

| | Consumer demand | | | | Investment | | | | | |
|---|---|---|---|---|---|---|---|---|---|---|
| | Total retail sales (volume) | Non-food retail sales (volume) | New car registrations | Changes in hire purchase debt total[1] | Capital expenditure of | | Engineering new home orders[2] | Housing: new starts | | Investment in stocks (manufacturing) |
| | | | | | Manufacturing industry | Distribution and services industries | | Private | Public | |
| | Up to 1980, 1976 = 100 From 1981, 1978 = 100 | | Thousands, monthly averages | £ million, end of period | £ million at 1975 prices | | 1975 = 100 | Thousands | | £ million at 1975 prices |
| 1972 | 98.7 | 95.8 | 139 | +438 | 3 370 | 4 045 | 99 | 228.0 | 123.0 | −288 |
| 1973 | 103.1 | 103.8 | 137 | +444 | 3 440 | 4 519 | 121 | 215.7 | 112.8 | 1 170 |
| 1974 | 101.9 | 101.9 | 103 | −164 | 3 782 | 4 477 | 102 | 105.9 | 146.1 | 1 281 |
| 1975 | 100.1 | 99.6 | 97 | −13 | 3 522 | 3 861 | 83 | 149.1 | 173.8 | −1 101 |
| 1976 | 100.0 | 100.0 | 105 | +348 | 3 326 | 3 959 | 87 | 154.7 | 170.8 | 363 |
| 1977 | 98.3 | 97.7 | 107 | +890 | 3 476 | 4 466 | 93 | 134.8 | 132.1 | 640 |
| 1978 | 103.8 | 106.3 | 130 | +1 484 | 3 769 | 5 073 | 100 | 157.3 | 107.4 | 228 |
| 1979 1 | 105.8 | 109.0 | 130 | +286 | 988 | 1 411 | 94 | 28.0 | 18.2 | 10 |
| 2 | 113.0 | 119.7 | 175 | +468 | 987 | 1 544 | 102 | 35.5 | 20.9 | 21 |
| 3 | 106.6 | 109.7 | 112 | +448 | 989 | 1 513 | 101 | 38.1 | 19.9 | 183 |
| 4 | 109.1 | 112.8 | 141 | +552 | 1 006 | 1 534 | 102 | 42.4 | 22.2 | −21 |
| 1980 1 | 110.2 | 113.9 | 140 | +489 | 955 | 1 535 | 97 | 30.1 | 18.2 | −120 |
| 2 | 109.2 | 112.6 | 119 | +310 | 914 | 1 553 | 92 | 25.2 | 14.2 | −101 |
| 3 | 108.9 | 113.9 | 121 | +215 | 895 | 1 571 | 83 | 21.4 | 13.2 | −322 |
| 4 | 109.0 | 113.4 | 116 | +123 | 810 | 1 653 | 79 | 21.3 | 10.4 | −650 |
| 1981 1 | 106.6 | 104.2 | 121 | +99 | 777 | 1 537 | 95 | 31.3 | 8.8 | −362 |
| 2 | 104.7 | 102.3 | 119 | +83 | 756 | 1 565 | 86 | 28.5 | 8.4 | −398 |
| 3 | 105.5 | 103.4 | 121 | +169 | 705 | 1 644 | 90 | 30.3 | 8.9 | −158 |
| 4 | 105.4 | 102.4 | 129 | +292 | 699 | 1 674 | 86 | 25.7 | 10.8 | −97 |
| 1982 1 | 106.6 | 105.2 | 118 | +331 | 696 | 1 700 | 87 | 37.6 | 15.5 | 8 |
| 2 | 106.2 | 104.3 | 117 | +261 | 660 | 1 639 | 85 | 33.9 | 12.4 | −9 |
| 3 | 108.7 | 108.4 | 131 | +575 | 662 | 1 716 | | 37.4 | 12.1 | −334 |
| % change latest quarter: | | | | | | | | | | |
| on previous quarter | +2.4 | +3.9 | +12.0 | | +0.3 | +4.7 | −2.3 | +10.3 | −2.4 | |
| on a year earlier | +3.0 | +4.8 | +8.3 | | −6.1 | +4.4 | −1.2 | +23.4 | +36.0 | |

1. Including further interest payments due over the whole period of the loans.
2. Net of cancellations.
Sources: *Economic Trends; Monthly Digest of Statistics.*

## Table D. Production and manpower

| | GDP average estimate[1] | GDP per person employed[2] | Index of industrial production | Index of manufacturing production | Unemployed | Unfilled vacancies for adults | Employment in production industries | Employment in manufacturing industries | Hours of overtime worked in manufacturing industries |
|---|---|---|---|---|---|---|---|---|---|
| | 1975 = 100 | | | | Thousands | | 1975 = 100 | | Million per week |
| 1972 | 96.0 | 100.0 | 101.9 | 100.0 | 816 | 145 | 103.0 | 103.9 | 12.51 |
| 1973 | 102.8 | 103.7 | 109.4 | 108.4 | 581 | 304 | 104.4 | 104.4 | 15.44 |
| 1974 | 101.1 | 101.5 | 105.1 | 106.6 | 571 | 298 | 104.1 | 104.7 | 16.53 |
| 1975 | 100.0 | 100.0 | 100.0 | 100.0 | 890 | 148 | 100.0 | 100.0 | 13.62 |
| 1976 | 102.6 | 102.6 | 102.1 | 101.4 | 1 223 | 120 | 97.3 | 96.9 | 14.00 |
| 1977 | 105.3 | 105.2 | 106.1 | 103.0 | 1 323 | 156 | 96.9 | 97.2 | 15.58 |
| 1978 | 108.7 | 108.2 | 110.3 | 104.0 | 1 316 | 210 | 96.8 | 96.7 | 15.50 |
| 1979  1 | 108.5 | 108.0 | 110.5 | 102.4 | 1 282 | 231 | 96.6 | 95.9 | 15.04 |
| 2 | 112.2 | 111.8 | 115.7 | 107.5 | 1 244 | 250 | 96.5 | 95.7 | 15.61 |
| 3 | 110.9 | 109.8 | 113.1 | 103.3 | 1 219 | 248 | 96.3 | 95.3 | 13.87 |
| 4 | 110.9 | 110.4 | 112.8 | 104.1 | 1 225 | 230 | 95.6 | 94.4 | 14.98 |
| 1980  1 | 110.2 | 109.9 | 110.4 | 100.4 | 1 299 | 193 | 94.5 | 93.2 | 14.15 |
| 2 | 108.9 | 109.1 | 107.4 | 97.4 | 1 428 | 159 | 93.1 | 91.4 | 12.36 |
| 3 | 106.8 | 108.5 | 104.1 | 93.8 | 1 646 | 121 | 90.8 | 88.7 | 10.73 |
| 4 | 106.1 | 108.5 | 101.5 | 90.1 | 1 931 | 99 | 88.3 | 85.7 | 8.86 |
| 1981  1 | 105.8 | 109.6 | 100.2 | 88.9 | 2 189 | 98 | 86.0 | 83.3 | 8.49 |
| 2 | 105.1 | 110.6 | 99.9 | 89.3 | 2 386 | 89 | 84.1 | 81.3 | 8.75 |
| 3 | 104.8 | 112.6 | 100.5 | 89.9 | 2 542 | 96 | 82.4 | 79.7 | 9.66 |
| 4 | 105.8 | 113.8 | 101.0 | 89.6 | 2 651 | 104 | 81.2 | 78.7 | 9.87 |
| 1982  1 | 105.9 | 114.1 | 100.7 | 89.2 | 2 713 | 112 | 80.0 | 77.6 | 10.08 |
| 2 | 106.0 | 115.1 | 100.9 | 88.9 | 2 769 | 107 | 79.0 | 76.5 | 9.87 |
| 3 | 106.0 | | 101.0 | 88.8 | 2 872 | 111 | 77.9 | 75.3 | 10.03 |
| % change latest quarter: | | | | | | | | | |
| on previous quarter | +0.1 | | +0.1 | -0.1 | | | -1.4 | -1.6 | +1.6 |
| on a year earlier | +0.5 | | +0.5 | -1.2 | | | -5.5 | -5.5 | +3.8 |

1. Average of expenditure, income and output data.
2. Based on output estimate of GDP.
Sources: *Economic Trends; Department of Employment Gazette.*

## Table E.  Domestic finance

| | Domestic credit expansion | Change in money supply Sterling M3 | General government borrowing requirement* | Sterling lending to the private sector by banks | Net increase in building society shares and deposits | Building society commitments to mortgages | Government securities-calculated redemption yields*[1] Short-dated | Medium-dated | Long-dated | Local authority deposits 3 months rates* | Covered comparison between local authority and Euro-dollar 3 months rates*[2] |
|---|---|---|---|---|---|---|---|---|---|---|---|
| | £ million | | | | £ million | | % per annum | | | % per annum at end of period | % per annum at end of period |
| 1971 | 988 | 2 459 | 1 313 | 1 856 | 2 034 | 3 012 | 6.68 | 8.24 | 8.90 | 4.56 | −0.64 |
| 1972 | 6 856 | 4 927 | 2 114 | 6 433 | 2 193 | 3 801 | 7.68 | 8.45 | 8.97 | 8.75 | −0.72 |
| 1973 | 8 782 | 6 702 | 3 679 | 7 129 | 2 163 | 3 255 | 10.45 | 10.65 | 10.78 | 16.06 | −0.82 |
| 1974 | 6 895 | 3 255 | 5 684 | 3 435 | 1 992 | 3 114 | 12.51 | 14.21 | 14.77 | 13.25 | −5.15 |
| 1975 | 4 530 | 2 331 | 9 974 | −371 | 4 173 | 5 301 | 11.48 | 13.18 | 14.39 | 11.31 | — |
| 1976 | 7 474 | 3 565 | 7 889 | 3 464 | 3 405 | 6 090 | 12.06 | 13.61 | 14.43 | 14.88 | −0.41 |
| 1977 | 1 130 | 4 130 | 4 652 | 3 188 | 6 099 | 7 524 | 10.08 | 12.02 | 12.73 | 6.75 | 0.16 |
| 1978 | 8 096 | 6 772 | 9 030 | 4 698 | 4 822 | 8 710 | 11.32 | 12.12 | 12.47 | 12.44 | −0.33 |
| 1979 1 | 1 406 | 945 | 1 248 | 2 338 | 1 348 | 2 307 | 12.71 | 13.16 | 13.32 | 12.44 | 0.21 |
| 2 | 2 667 | 1 925 | 3 574 | 2 239 | 1 330 | 2 275 | 11.23 | 11.89 | 12.10 | 14.13 | −0.20 |
| 3 | 2 928 | 1 657 | 3 474 | 1 970 | 1 591 | 2 228 | 12.11 | 12.34 | 12.38 | 14.25 | −0.03 |
| 4 | 2 398 | 2 112 | 3 895 | 2 038 | 1 500 | 2 309 | 14.52 | 14.33 | 14.14 | 17.22 | 0.32 |
| 1980 1 | 1 738 | 1 564 | −568 | 3 155 | 1 497 | 2 303 | 15.10 | 14.70 | 14.44 | 18.81 | −0.03 |
| 2 | 3 616 | 3 275 | 5 160 | 2 428 | 1 619 | 2 325 | 14.03 | 14.10 | 14.02 | 17.00 | 0.10 |
| 3 | 6 494 | 2 919 | 3 559 | 2 696 | 1 976 | 2 577 | 13.11 | 13.42 | 13.34 | 15.37 | 0.09 |
| 4 | 3 559 | 3 291 | 4 786 | 1 746 | 2 067 | 3 023 | 13.11 | 13.44 | 13.34 | 14.75 | 0.34 |
| 1981 1 | 1 232 | 1 131 | 402 | 2 062 | 2 078 | 3 293 | 13.14 | 13.82 | 13.84 | 12.78 | 0.14 |
| 2 | 4 036 | 3 055 | 7 738 | 800 | 2 063 | 3 151 | 13.70 | 14.25 | 14.17 | 12.53 | 0.11 |
| 3 | 6 030 | 3 296 | 2 537 | 3 068 | 1 675 | 2 837 | 15.20 | 15.44 | 15.27 | 15.69 | −0.47 |
| 4 | 2 350 | 1 748 | 538 | 5 169 | 1 380 | 2 667 | 16.57 | 16.02 | 15.68 | 15.75 | 0.60 |
| 1982 1 | 3 196 | 1 638 | −2 267 | 5 830 | 2 207 | 3 324 | 15.34 | 15.01 | 14.68 | 13.66 | 0.22 |
| 2 | 4 571 | 2 097 | 3 228 | 3 382 | 2 395 | 4 032 | 13.91 | 13.95 | 13.74 | 13.13 | 0.25 |
| 3 | 4 844 | 2 914 | 1 743 | | 2 519 | 4 078 | 11.61 | 12.36 | 12.28 | 10.88 | 0.13 |
| % change latest quarter: on previous quarter | | | | | +5.2 | +1.1 | | | | | |
| on a year earlier | | | | | +50.4 | +43.7 | | | | | |

* Not seasonally adjusted.
1. Average of Wednesday yields throughout the period.
2. Difference between the local authority rate net of the cost of forward cover and the Euro-dollar rate. A plus indicates that the net local authority rate is above in the Euro-dollar and a minus that it is below.
   Sources:  Bank of England Quarterly Bulletin; Financial Statistics.

## Table F.  Wages, prices and external position

| | Weekly wage rates* | Average earnings | Wholesale prices manufacturing output for home market*1 | Retail price index* | Export unit values* | Import unit values*2 | Exports3 (fob) | Imports4 (fob) | Visible balance | Current balance | Total currency flow* |
|---|---|---|---|---|---|---|---|---|---|---|---|
| | 31st July 1972 = 100 | Jan. 1976 = 100 | 1975 = 100 | 1975 = 100 | 1975 = 100 | 1975 = 100 | £ million | £ million | £ million | £ million | £ million |
| 1972 | 101.3 | .. | 40.5 | 63.6 | 56.8 | 46.9 | 9 437 | 10 185 | −748 | +247 | −1 265 |
| 1973 | 115.2 | .. | 53.1 | 69.4 | 64.0 | 60.0 | 11 937 | 14 523 | −2 586 | −981 | −771 |
| 1974 | 138.0 | .. | 86.8 | 80.5 | 81.6 | 87.7 | 16 394 | 21 745 | −5 351 | −3 273 | −1 646 |
| 1975 | 178.7 | .. | 100.0 | 100.0 | 100.0 | 100.0 | 19 330 | 22 663 | −3 333 | −1 521 | −1 465 |
| 1976 | 213.2 | 106.1 | 116.9 | 116.5 | 119.6 | 122.2 | 25 191 | 29 120 | −3 929 | −875 | −3 628 |
| 1977 | 227.3 | 115.6 | 138.0 | 135.0 | 141.5 | 141.3 | 31 728 | 34 012 | −2 284 | −22 | +7 362 |
| 1978 | 259.3 | 130.6 | 150.9 | 146.2 | 155.5 | 146.8 | 35 063 | 36 605 | −1 542 | +1 018 | −1 126 |
| 1979  1 | 284.9 | 141.0 | 160.0 | 155.0 | 166.0 | 154.2 | 8 310 | 9 736 | −1 426 | −571 | +684 |
| 2 | 292.2 | 146.6 | 167.3 | 160.7 | 169.2 | 158.8 | 10 765 | 11 280 | −515 | −6 | +758 |
| 3 | 299.9 | 153.9 | 176.6 | 171.4 | 173.2 | 162.0 | 10 488 | 11 241 | −753 | +34 | +297 |
| 4 | 315.3 | 161.8 | 182.5 | 176.2 | 178.8 | 172.8 | 11 115 | 11 879 | −764 | −310 | −29 |
| 1980  1 | 334.9 | 168.8 | 193.7 | 184.6 | 187.2 | 185.3 | 11 876 | 12 261 | −385 | +68 | +509 |
| 2 | 348.3 | 178.0 | 200.8 | 195.3 | 191.6 | 185.4 | 11 915 | 12 237 | −322 | −39 | +246 |
| 3 | 357.4 | 188.1 | 206.0 | 199.4 | 195.5 | 185.4 | 11 707 | 11 087 | 620 | +943 | +279 |
| 4 | 366.6 | 193.3 | 208.6 | 203.2 | 196.8 | 187.1 | 11 891 | 10 626 | 1 265 | +1 893 | +158 |
| 1981  1 | 377.0 | 196.7 | 213.8 | 208.0 | 199.3 | 189.8 | 11 769 | 10 092 | 1 677 | +2 392 | +161 |
| 2 | 385.5 | 201.2 | 218.8 | 218.1 | 204.2 | 199.1 | 12 253 | 11 121 | 1 132 | +1 967 | −165 |
| 3 | 391.1 | 209.6 | 223.7 | 221.9 | 211.2 | 209.9 | 13 191 | 13 511 | −320 | +160 | −709 |
| 4 | 396.4 | 214.8 | 229.4 | 227.4 | 217.1 | 217.7 | 13 858 | 13 368 | 490 | +1 483 | −132 |
| 1982  1 | 404.4 | 218.5 | 234.5 | 231.1 | 219.4 | 217.0 | 13 279 | 12 956 | 323 | +720 | −31 |
| 2 | 411.6 | 221.5 | 237.1 | 238.5 | 220.3 | 217.9 | 13 745 | 13 642 | 103 | +887 | −661 |
| 3 | 414.8 | 227.4 | 241.1 | 239.5 | 223.5 | 222.1 | 13 693 | 13 325 | 368 | +968 | +247 |
| % change latest quarter: on previous quarter | +0.8 | +2.7 | +1.7 | +0.4 | +1.5 | +1.9 | | | | | |
| on a year earlier | +6.1 | +8.5 | +7.8 | +7.9 | +5.8 | +5.8 | | | | | |

\* Not seasonally adjusted.
1. Excluding food, drink, tobacco.
2. Excluding United States military aircraft.
3. Including balance of payments adjustments and allowance for factors affecting recording.
4. Includes payments for United States military aircraft and other balance of payments adjustments.
Sources: *Economic Trends; Monthly Digest of Statistics.*

| | | 1980 | 1981 | Q1 |
|---|---|---|---|---|
| 1. | **Current balance** | +2 865 | +6 122 | +2 4 |
| | *Investment and other capital transactions* | | | |
| 2. | Official long-term capital | −91 | −336 | • −128 |
| 3. | Overseas investment in UK public sector | +589 | +188 | +82 |
| | British government stocks[2] | +571 | +201 | +89 |
| | Other | +18 | −13 | −7 |
| 4. | Overseas investment in UK private sector | +4 654 | +3 168 | +348 |
| 5. | UK private investment overseas | −8 204 | −10 597 | −3 010 |
| 6. | Foreign currency borrowing or lending abroad by UK banks | +2 018 | +1 404 | −580 |
| | *Exchange reserves in sterling[3]* | | | |
| 7. | British government stocks | +945 | +258 | −95 |
| 8. | Banking and money market liabilities | +317 | −118 | +187 |
| 9. | Other external banking and money market liabilities in sterling | +2 558 | +2 607 | +301 |
| 10. | External sterling lending by UK banks | −2 500 | −2 943 | −1 229 |
| 11. | Other external borrowing or lending | −766 | +36 | +245 |
| 12. | Import credit[4] | −268 | +115 | −83 |
| 13. | Export credit[4] | −902 | −999 | +71 |
| 14. | Other short-term transactions | −217 | +80 | −130 |
| 15. | Total investment and other capital transactions | −1 867 | −7 138 | −4 0 |
| 16. | Balancing item | +194 | +171 | +1 7 |
| 17. | **Balance for official financing** | +1 192 | −845 | +1 |
| 18. | Allocation of Special Drawing Rights | +180 | +158 | +1. |
| 19. | Gold subscription to IMF | — | — | — |
| 20. | **Total-rows** 17 to 19 | +1 372 | −687 | +3 |
| | *Official financing* | | | |
| | Net transactions with overseas monetary authorities | | | |
| 21. | IMF | −140 | −145 | −33 |
| 22. | Other monetary authorities | — | — | — |
| 23. | Foreign currency borrowing by HM Government | −629 | −1 234 | — |
| 24. | Foreign currency borrowing by public sector under exchange cover scheme | −312 | −353 | +33 |
| 25. | Drawings on (+) additions to (−) official reserves[5] | −291 | +2 419 | −319 |
| 26. | **Total official financing** | −1 372 | +687 | −3 |

1. The sum of items 1-5 equals the total formerly known as the "basic balance"; the remainder (except for item 16) makes up the total formerly known as "monetary movements".
2. Holdings of British government stocks by non-residents other than overseas monetary authorities, which are included as exchange reserves in sterling.
3. Sterling reserves of overseas countries and international organisations (other than IMF) as reported by banks, etc., in the United Kingdom. Exclude other official funds such as trust, pension and other earmarked funds, holdings of equities and funds held locally with commercial banks, movements in which are included in items 3, 4 and 9.
4. Excluding trade credit between "related" firms (part of items 4 and 5). After deducting advance and progress payments to suppliers.
5. Valued in sterling at transactions rates of exchange.
*Source: Bank of England Quarterly Bulletin.*

| | 1981 | | | 1982 | | |
|---|---|---|---|---|---|---|
| | Q2 | Q3 | Q4 | Q1 | Q2 | Q3 |
| | +1 570 | +399 | +1 714 | +941 | +387 | +1 186 |
| | −111 | −5 | −92 | −210 | −23 | −2 |
| | −156 | −11 | +273 | −52 | −106 | — |
| | −157 | −6 | +275 | −48 | +11 | — |
| | +1 | −5 | −2 | −4 | −117 | — |
| | +1 262 | +757 | +801 | +1 094 | +710 | +694 |
| | −2 399 | −2 176 | −3 012 | −3 010 | −2 313 | −2 191 |
| | −751 | +119 | +2 616 | +1 646 | +535 | +1 179 |
| | +152 | +95 | +106 | −46 | +82 | −165 |
| | +21 | +49 | −375 | +511 | −301 | +345 |
| | +902 | +1 015 | +389 | +1 148 | +1 492 | +1 033 |
| | −433 | −796 | −485 | −1 097 | +208 | −1 337 |
| | −588 | −105 | +484 | +353 | +36 | +313 |
| | +52 | +213 | −67 | −93 | −10 | −19 |
| | −216 | −269 | −585 | −152 | −186 | −333 |
| | +382 | +56 | −228 | −239 | −39 | +150 |
| | −1 883 | −1 058 | −175 | −146 | +85 | −334 |
| | +148 | −50 | −1 671 | −826 | −1 133 | −605 |
| | −165 | −709 | −132 | −31 | −661 | +247 |
| | — | — | — | — | — | — |
| | — | — | — | — | — | — |
| | −165 | −709 | −132 | −31 | −661 | +247 |
| | −35 | −38 | −39 | −38 | −60 | −32 |
| | — | — | — | — | — | — |
| | −942 | −292 | — | — | — | — |
| | −306 | −128 | +48 | +58 | +22 | +73 |
| | +1 448 | +1 167 | +123 | +11 | +699 | −288 |
| | +165 | +709 | +132 | +31 | +661 | −247 |

## Table H. Foreign assets and liabilities

| | Effective exchange rate | Official reserves[3] | | Sterling balances | | | Outstanding official borrowing from abroad[4] | |
|---|---|---|---|---|---|---|---|---|
| | | Total | of which: Convertible currencies | Official | | Other holders | Total | of which: IMF[2] |
| | | | | Total | of which: Oil-exporting countries | | | |
| | 1970 = 100 | $ million, end of period | | £ million, end of period | | | $ million, end of period | |
| 1972 | 96.6 | 5 646 | 4 063 | 3 618 | : | 2 291 | 366 | — |
| 1973 | 85.6 | 6 476 | 4 725 | 3 689 | 959 | 2 284 | 2 982 | — |
| 1974 | 82.1 | 6 789 | 4 823 | 4 634 | 3 101 | 2 500 | 7 092 | — |
| 1975 | 75.8 | 5 429 | 3 335 | 4 102 | 2 839 | 3 228 | 8 921 | |
| 1976 | 64.7 | 4 129 | 2 513 | 2 647 | 1 421 | 3 484 | 14 160 | 2 051 |
| 1977 | 61.7 | 20 557 | 19 015 | 2 852 | 1 360 | 4 965 | 18 042 | 4 029 |
| 1978 | 61.7 | 15 694 | 14 230 | 2 633 | | 5 258 | 15 847 | 2 152 |
| 1979 1 | 62.0 | 21 947 | 16 885 | 2 771 | 1 072 | 5 728 | 16 551 | 2 300 |
| 2 | 65.4 | 22 070 | 16 911 | 2 868 | 1 139 | 6 086 | 15 104 | 1 209 |
| 3 | 68.4 | 22 692 | 18 313 | 3 268 | 1 335 | 6 536 | 14 783 | 1 128 |
| 4 | 66.0 | 22 538 | 18 034 | 3 320 | 1 205 | 7 838 | 14 585 | 1 048 |
| 1980 1 | 69.3 | 26 963 | 18 325 | 3 785 | 1 670 | 8 007 | 13 921 | 938 |
| 2 | 70.8 | 28 172 | 19 500 | 4 139 | 1 902 | 8 990 | 13 676 | 860 |
| 3 | 72.3 | 27 637 | 18 855 | 4 496 | 2 105 | 9 814 | 12 481 | 782 |
| 4 | 75.7 | 27 476 | 18 621 | 4 669 | 2 238 | 10 309 | 11 986 | 704 |
| 1981 1 | 77.7 | 28 212 | 18 546 | 4 761 | 2 465 | 10 610 | 11 893 | 612 |
| 2 | 75.0 | 25 631 | 15 975 | 4 934 | 2 602 | 11 512 | 9 231 | 535 |
| 3 | 69.5 | 23 696 | 13 848 | 5 078 | 2 615 | 12 527 | 8 359 | 459 |
| 4 | 68.1 | 23 347 | 13 457 | 4 746 | 2 470 | 13 434 | 8 372 | 382 |
| 1982 1 | 69.3 | 18 969 | 11 949 | 5 211 | 2 551 | 14 591 | 8 131 | 278 |
| 2 | 68.9 | 17 703 | 10 741 | 4 992 | 2 473 | 16 096 | 8 065 | 172 |
| 3 | 69.7 | 18 299 | 11 257 | 5 172 | 2 352 | 17 136 | 8 137 | 115 |

*Memorandum item:* Schedule of capital repayments of certain public sector foreign currency liabilities outstanding at end-1981 ($ billion).

| 1982 | 1983 | 1984 | 1985 | 1986 | 1987 | 1988 | 1989 | 1990 | 1991 | 1992 onwards | Total |
|---|---|---|---|---|---|---|---|---|---|---|---|
| 1.7 | 0.9 | 1.6 | 1.2 | 1.2 | 1.4 | 1.2 | 0.9 | 0.7 | 0.7 | 2.8 | 14.3 |

1. The borrowing included is that recorded as official financing in the balance of payments accounts.

2. Drawings from the IMF, net of repayments by the United Kingdom, and drawings of sterling from the IMF by other countries; excludes interest and charges in sterling.

3. From end-March 1979 the rates at which the reserves are valued are to be revised annually. Gold is valued at $35 per fine ounce until end-November 1971, then at $38 per fine ounce until end-January 1973 and at $42.2222 per fine ounce until end-March 1979. Special drawing rights are valued at SDR 1=$1 until end-November 1971, at SDR 1=$1.08571 until end-January 1973 and at SDR 1=$1.20635 to end-March 1979. Convertible currencies are valued at middle or central rates from end-December 1971 to end-March 1979. The basis of valuation announced in 1979 was modified in March 1980. In 1979, gold was valued at the average of the London fixing price for the three months up to end-March, less 25%; from end-March 1980 it is to be valued at that price or at 75% of its final fixing price on the last working day in March, whichever is the lower. Special drawing rights and convertible currencies are valued from end-March 1979 at the average of their exchange rates against the US dollar in the three months to end-March, with the alternative, from end-March 1980, of their actual US dollar values on the last working day of March, whichever is lower. From July 1979, convertible currencies include European currency units (ECUs) acquired from swaps with the European Monetary Co-operation Fund. These are valued at the average of the $/ECU or $/European unit of account exchange rates in the three months to end-March or (from end-March 1980) at the rate applicable on the last working day in March, whichever is lower. Until March 1980 this valuation differed from that used for monthly reserve announcements, where ECUs were valued at the market rate applicable for each swap.

4. From end-March 1979 the rates at which outstanding borrowing is valued are to be revised annually on the same basis as the reserves. The effect of the 1979 revaluation was to increase the level of borrowings at end-March by $576 million (IMF +$148 million and other public sector under the exchange cover schemes +$428 million).

Source: Bank of England Quarterly Bulletin.

## Table I. Foreign trade by area
### Million US dollars, monthly averages

| | 1968 | 1969 | 1970 | 1971 | 1972 | 1973 | 1974 | 1975 | 1976 | 1977 | 1978 | 1979 | 1980 | 1981 |
|---|---|---|---|---|---|---|---|---|---|---|---|---|---|---|
| **Imports, cif** | | | | | | | | | | | | | | |
| Total OECD | 1 050 | 1 100 | 1 240 | 1 382 | 1 659 | 2 303 | 3 032 | 3 078 | 3 209 | 3 781 | 4 951 | 6 637 | 7 564 | 6 708 |
| North America | 314 | 326 | 371 | 351 | 371 | 480 | 633 | 593 | 630 | 716 | 854 | 1 100 | 1 452 | 1 272 |
| OECD Europe | 630 | 661 | 748 | 887 | 1 109 | 1 606 | 2 175 | 2 257 | 2 351 | 2 800 | 3 766 | 5 117 | 5 604 | 4 931 |
| EEC | 415 | 430 | 488 | 593 | 733 | 1 059 | 1 510 | 1 626 | 1 703 | 2 043 | 2 653 | 3 694 | 4 060 | 3 628 |
| Centrally planned economies | 68 | 74 | 80 | 78 | 89 | 122 | 146 | 138 | 169 | 197 | 207 | 271 | 278 | 168 |
| Developing countries | 403 | 423 | 430 | 478 | 503 | 711 | 1 241 | 1 111 | 1 185 | 1 191 | 1 253 | 1 546 | 2 002 | 1 555 |
| of which: OPEC | 147 | 153 | 160 | 212 | 210 | 295 | 725 | 578 | 611 | 530 | 538 | 580 | 826 | 603 |
| **Exports, fob** | | | | | | | | | | | | | | |
| Total OECD | 868 | 990 | 1 102 | 1 260 | 1 426 | 1 827 | 2 286 | 2 404 | 2 633 | 3 296 | 4 081 | 5 526 | 6 941 | 6 047 |
| North America | 235 | 243 | 246 | 291 | 332 | 394 | 441 | 425 | 463 | 555 | 678 | 854 | 1 055 | 1 182 |
| OECD Europe | 529 | 633 | 731 | 832 | 960 | 1 260 | 1 615 | 1 756 | 1 974 | 2 518 | 3 135 | 4 361 | 5 562 | 4 578 |
| EEC | 346 | 410 | 471 | 540 | 612 | 821 | 1 077 | 1 178 | 1 371 | 1 753 | 2 256 | 3 162 | 4 081 | 3 552 |
| Centrally planned economies | 53 | 58 | 62 | 58 | 64 | 84 | 101 | 123 | 109 | 131 | 171 | 210 | 255 | 192 |
| Developing countries | 306 | 354 | 375 | 458 | 468 | 542 | 723 | 981 | 1 007 | 1 267 | 1 598 | 1 679 | 2 180 | 2 051 |
| of which: OPEC | 66 | 83 | 85 | 107 | 122 | 151 | 219 | 389 | 440 | 580 | 703 | 603 | 881 | 923 |

*Source:* OECD, *Foreign Trade Statistics, Series A.*

*BASIC STATISTICS :*

*INTERNATIONAL COMPARISONS*

| | Reference period | Units |
|---|---|---|
| POPULATION | Mid-1980 | Thousands |
|     Inhabitants per sq. km of land area | » | Number |
|     Net average annual increase | Mid-1970 to Mid-1980 | % |
| EMPLOYMENT   Total civilian | 1980 | Thousands |
|     *of which:* Agriculture, forestry, fishing | » | % of total |
|               Industry[4] | » | » |
|               Other | » | » |
| GROSS DOMESTIC PRODUCT at market prices | 1980 | US $ billion[11] |
|     Average annual volume growth[6] | 1975 to 1980 | % |
|     Per capita | 1980 | US $[11] |
| GROSS FIXED CAPITAL FORMATION | 1980 | % of GDP |
|     *of which:* Transport, machinery and equipment | 1979 | » |
|              Residential construction | » | » |
|     Average annual volume growth[6] | 1975 to 1980 | % |
| GROSS SAVING RATIO[12] | 1980 | % of GDP |
| GENERAL GOVERNMENT | | |
|     Current expenditure on goods and services | 1979 | % of GDP |
|     Current disbursements[13] | » | » |
|     Current receipts | » | » |
| NET OFFICIAL DEVELOPMENT ASSISTANCE | 1980 | % of GNP |
| INDICATORS OF LIVING STANDARDS | | |
|     Private consumption per capita | 1980 | US $[11] |
|     Passenger cars, per 1 000 inhabitants | 1978 | Number |
|     Telephones, per 1 000 inhabitants | 1979 | » |
|     Television sets, per 1 000 inhabitants | 1977 | » |
|     Doctors, per 1 000 inhabitants | 1977 | » |
|     Full-time school enrolment[15] | 1979 | % of age group |
|     Infant mortality[17] | 1980 | Number |
| WAGES AND PRICES | Average annual increase | |
|     Hourly earnings in industry[18] | 1975 to 1980 | % |
|     Consumer prices | » | % |
| FOREIGN TRADE | | |
|     Exports of goods, fob | 1980 | US $ million[11] |
|         As percentage of GDP | » | % |
|         Average annual volume increase | 1975 to 1980 | % |
|     Imports of goods, cif | 1980 | US $ million[11] |
|         As percentage of GDP | » | % |
|         Average annual volume increase | 1975 to 1980 | % |
| TOTAL OFFICIAL RESERVES[24] | End-1980 | US $ million |
|     As percentage of imports of goods | In 1980 | % |

1. Partly from national sources.
2. Total resident population.
3. Private and socialised sector.
4. According to the definition used in OECD: Labour Force Statistics: mining, manufacturing, construction and utilities (electricity, gas and water).
5. Social product.
6. At constant prices.
7. Including Luxembourg.

| Australia | Portugal | Spain | Sweden | Switzer-land | Turkey | United Kingdom | United States | Yugo-slavia[1] |
|---|---|---|---|---|---|---|---|---|
| 14 616 | 9 966 | 37 381 | 8 316 | 6 373 | 45 078 | 56 010 | 227 658 | 22 340 |
| 2 | 108 | 74 | 18 | 154 | 58 | 230 | 24 | 87 |
| 1.4 | 1.0 | 1.1 | 0.3 | 0.2 | 2.4 | 0.1 | 1.1 | 0.9 |
| | | | | | | | | |
| 6 242 | 3 951 | 11 254 | 4 232 | 3 012 | 14 610 | 24 397 | 97 270 | 9 690[3] |
| 6.5 | 28.3 | 18.9 | 5.6 | 7.2 | 60.4 | 2.6 | 3.6 | .. |
| 31.0 | 35.7 | 36.1 | 32.2 | 39.5 | 16.3 | 38.0 | 30.6 | 22.3 |
| 62.5 | 36.0 | 45.0 | 62.2 | 53.3 | 23.3 | 59.4 | 65.8 | 41.9 |
| | | | | | | | | |
| 140.0 | 24.1 | 211.1 | 122.8 | 101.5 | 52.9 | 522.9 | 2 587.1 | 56.2[5] |
| 2.5 | 5.2 | 2.2 | 1.2 | 1.6 | 2.8 | 1.6 | 3.9 | 5.6 |
| 9 580 | 2 430 | 5 650 | 14 760 | 15 920 | 1 170 | 9 340 | 11 360 | 2 516 |
| | | | | | | | | |
| 22.8 | 20.9 | 19.6 | 20.3 | 23.8 | 18.0 | 17.8 | 18.2 | 35.5 |
| .. | 7.1 | 6.9[19] | 7.3 | 7.1 | .. | 9.3 | 7.4 | .. |
| 4.2[10] | 3.7 | .. | 5.0 | .. | 3.8 | 3.0 | 4.8 | 7.2 |
| 1.6 | 4.7 | −0.9 | −0.2 | 2.2 | −0.2 | 0.3 | 3.3 | 5.7 |
| | | | | | | | | |
| 21.4[10] | 20.5 | 18.9 | 17.3 | 26.7 | 16.6 | 19.2 | 18.3 | 37.0 |
| | | | | | | | | |
| 16.2 | 14.8 | 10.8 | 28.4 | 12.9 | 13.7 | 20.0 | 17.4 | 17.6 |
| 29.6[10] | 30.7 | 26.7 | 56.8 | 29.9 | 23.4 | 40.0 | 31.5 | .. |
| 32.5[10] | 26.9 | 27.5 | 57.4 | 33.2 | 23.8 | 39.0 | 32.5 | .. |
| | | | | | | | | |
| 0.5 | .. | .. | 0.8 | 0.2 | .. | 0.3 | 0.3 | .. |
| | | | | | | | | |
| 5 800 | 1 790 | 3 950 | 7 630 | 10 128 | 851 | 5 581 | 7 370 | 1 343 |
| 479 | 118 | 178 | 345 | 324 | 11[14] | 256 | 536 | 85 |
| 440[19] | 132 | 294 | 772 | 700 | 39 | 480 | 793 | 79[19] |
| 351[14] | 76[14] | 185[14] | 363[14] | 285[14] | 44[14] | 324 | 571[20] | 199 |
| 1.5[14] | 1.5 | 1.8 | 1.8[14] | 2.0 | 0.6 | 1.5 | 1.7 | 1.3 |
| 44.4 | 33.4[14] | 41.3[19] | 56.3[14] | 70.1[22] | 12.7[20] | 46.2[22] | 75.0 | 52.2 |
| 11.0 | 26.0[23] | 11.1 | 6.7 | 8.5[23] | .. | 11.8 | 12.6 | 33.4[19] |
| | | | | | | | | |
| 10.3 | 14.5 | 25.7 | 9.9 | 2.8 | 35.5 | 14.9 | 8.5 | 19.0 |
| 10.6 | 21.8 | 18.6 | 10.5 | 2.3 | 50.1 | 14.4 | 8.9 | 17.9 |
| | | | | | | | | |
| 22 068 | 4 644 | 20 820 | 30 924 | 29 616 | 2 748 | 115 176 | 220 704 | 8 568 |
| 15.8 | 19.3 | 9.8 | 25.3 | 29.9 | 5.2 | 22.4 | 8.6 | 15.2 |
| 3.7 | .. | 9.9[25] | 2.1 | 6.3 | 4.7 | 4.7 | 6.7 | 3.8 |
| 20 208 | 9 300 | 34 176 | 33 420 | 36 336 | 6 252 | 120 156 | 241 200 | 14 436 |
| 14.5 | 38.7 | 16.1 | 27.4 | 36.7 | 11.8 | 23.3 | 9.4 | 25.7 |
| 5.0 | .. | 0.7[25] | 0.8 | 9.0 | −4.1 | 3.9 | 6.7 | 0.5 |
| | | | | | | | | |
| 2 044 | 1 784 | 12 516 | 3 690 | 19 374 | 1 442 | 21 492 | 27 395 | 1 467 |
| 10.1 | 19.2 | 36.6 | 11.0 | 53.3 | 23.1 | 17.9 | 11.4 | 10.2 |

24. Gold included in reserves is valued at 35 SDR per ounce (see IMF, International Financial Statistics, series Total Reserves).
25. 1976 to 1980.

*Note:* Figures within brackets are estimates by the OECD Secretariat.

*Sources:* Common to all subjects and countries: OECD: Labour Force Statistics, Main Economic Indicators, National Accounts, Observer, Statistics of Foreign Trade (Series A); Statistical Office of the European Communities, Basic Statistics of the Community; IMF, International Financial Statistics; UN, Statistical Yearbook.
National sources have also been used when data are not available according to standard international definitions.

# OECD SALES AGENTS
# DÉPOSITAIRES DES PUBLICATIONS DE L'OCDE

**ARGENTINA – ARGENTINE**
Carlos Hirsch S.R.L., Florida 165, 4° Piso (Galería Guemes)
1333 BUENOS AIRES, Tel. 33.1787.2391 y 30.7122
**AUSTRALIA – AUSTRALIE**
Australia and New Zealand Book Company Pty, Ltd.,
10 Aquatic Drive, Frenchs Forest, N.S.W. 2086
P.O. Box 459, BROOKVALE, N.S.W. 2100
**AUSTRIA – AUTRICHE**
OECD Publications and Information Center
4 Simrockstrasse 5300 BONN. Tel. (0228) 21.60.45
Local Agent/Agent local :
Gerold and Co., Graben 31, WIEN 1. Tel. 52.22.35
**BELGIUM – BELGIQUE**
CCLS – LCLS
19, rue Plantin, 1070 BRUXELLES. Tel. 02.521.04.73
**BRAZIL – BRÉSIL**
Mestre Jou S.A., Rua Guaipa 518,
Caixa Postal 24090, 05089 SAO PAULO 10. Tel. 261.1920
Rua Senador Dantas 19 s/205-6, RIO DE JANEIRO GB.
Tel. 232.07.32
**CANADA**
Renouf Publishing Company Limited,
2182 St. Catherine Street West,
MONTRÉAL, Que. H3H 1M7. Tel. (514)937.3519
OTTAWA, Ont. K1P 5A6, 61 Sparks Street
**DENMARK – DANEMARK**
Munksgaard Export and Subscription Service
35, Nørre Søgade
DK 1370 KØBENHAVN K. Tel. +45.1.12.85.70
**FINLAND – FINLANDE**
Akateeminen Kirjakauppa
Keskuskatu 1, 00100 HELSINKI 10. Tel. 65.11.22
**FRANCE**
Bureau des Publications de l'OCDE,
2 rue André-Pascal, 75775 PARIS CEDEX 16. Tel. (1) 524.81.67
Principal correspondant :
13602 AIX-EN-PROVENCE : Librairie de l'Université.
Tel. 26.18.08
**GERMANY – ALLEMAGNE**
OECD Publications and Information Center
4 Simrockstrasse 5300 BONN Tel. (0228) 21.60.45
**GREECE – GRÈCE**
Librairie Kauffmann, 28 rue du Stade,
ATHÈNES 132. Tel. 322.21.60
**HONG-KONG**
Government Information Services,
Publications/Sales Section, Baskerville House,
2/F., 22 Ice House Street
**ICELAND – ISLANDE**
Snaebjörn Jönsson and Co., h.f.,
Hafnarstraeti 4 and 9, P.O.B. 1131, REYKJAVIK.
Tel. 13133/14281/11936
**INDIA – INDE**
Oxford Book and Stationery Co. :
NEW DELHI-1, Scindia House. Tel. 45896
CALCUTTA 700016, 17 Park Street. Tel. 240832
**INDONESIA – INDONÉSIE**
PDIN-LIPI, P.O. Box 3065/JKT., JAKARTA, Tel. 583467
**IRELAND – IRLANDE**
TDC Publishers – Library Suppliers
12 North Frederick Street, DUBLIN 1 Tel. 744835-749677
**ITALY – ITALIE**
Libreria Commissionaria Sansoni :
Via Lamarmora 45, 50121 FIRENZE. Tel. 579751/584468
Via Bartolini 29, 20155 MILANO. Tel. 365083
Sub-depositari :
Ugo Tassi
Via A. Farnese 28, 00192 ROMA. Tel. 310590
Editrice e Libreria Herder,
Piazza Montecitorio 120, 00186 ROMA. Tel. 6794628
Costantino Ercolano, Via Generale Orsini 46, 80132 NAPOLI. Tel.
405210
Libreria Hoepli, Via Hoepli 5, 20121 MILANO. Tel. 865446
Libreria Scientifica, Dott. Lucio de Biasio "Aeiou"
Via Meravigli 16, 20123 MILANO Tel. 807679
Libreria Zanichelli
Piazza Galvani 1/A, 40124 Bologna Tel. 237389
Libreria Lattes, Via Garibaldi 3, 10122 TORINO. Tel. 519274
La diffusione delle edizioni OCSE è inoltre assicurata dalle migliori
librerie nelle città più importanti.
**JAPAN – JAPON**
OECD Publications and Information Center,
Landic Akasaka Bldg., 2-3-4 Akasaka,
Minato-ku, TOKYO 107 Tel. 586.2016
**KOREA – CORÉE**
Pan Korea Book Corporation,
P.O. Box n° 101 Kwangwhamun, SÉOUL. Tel. 72.7369

**LEBANON – LIBAN**
Documenta Scientifica/Redico,
Edison Building, Bliss Street, P.O. Box 5641, BEIRUT.
Tel. 354429 – 344425
**MALAYSIA – MALAISIE**
and/et SINGAPORE - SINGAPOUR
University of Malaya Co-operative Bookshop Ltd.
P.O. Box 1127, Jalan Pantai Baru
KUALA LUMPUR. Tel. 51425, 54058, 54361
**THE NETHERLANDS – PAYS-BAS**
Staatsuitgeverij
Verzendboekhandel Chr. Plantijnstraat 1
Postbus 20014
2500 EA S-GRAVENHAGE. Tel. nr. 070.789911
Voor bestellingen: Tel. 070.789208
**NEW ZEALAND – NOUVELLE-ZÉLANDE**
Publications Section,
Government Printing Office Bookshops:
AUCKLAND: Retail Bookshop: 25 Rutland Street,
Mail Orders: 85 Beach Road, Private Bag C.P.O.
HAMILTON: Retail Ward Street,
Mail Orders, P.O. Box 857
WELLINGTON: Retail: Mulgrave Street (Head Office),
Cubacade World Trade Centre
Mail Orders: Private Bag
CHRISTCHURCH: Retail: 159 Hereford Street,
Mail Orders: Private Bag
DUNEDIN: Retail: Princes Street
Mail Order: P.O. Box 1104
**NORWAY – NORVÈGE**
J.G. TANUM A/S Karl Johansgate 43
P.O. Box 1177 Sentrum OSLO 1. Tel. (02) 80.12.60
**PAKISTAN**
Mirza Book Agency, 65 Shahrah Quaid-E-Azam, LAHORE 3.
Tel. 66839
**PHILIPPINES**
National Book Store, Inc.
Library Services Division, P.O. Box 1934, MANILA.
Tel. Nos. 49.43.06 to 09, 40.53.45, 49.45.12
**PORTUGAL**
Livraria Portugal, Rua do Carmo 70-74,
1117 LISBOA CODEX. Tel. 360582/3
**SPAIN – ESPAGNE**
Mundi-Prensa Libros, S.A.
Castelló 37, Apartado 1223, MADRID-1. Tel. 275.46.55
Libreria Bosch, Ronda Universidad 11, BARCELONA 7.
Tel. 317.53.08, 317.53.58
**SWEDEN – SUÈDE**
AB CE Fritzes Kungl Hovbokhandel,
Box 16 356, S 103 27 STH, Regeringsgatan 12,
DS STOCKHOLM. Tel. 08/23.89.00
**SWITZERLAND – SUISSE**
OECD Publications and Information Center
4 Simrockstrasse 5300 BONN. Tel. (0228) 21.60.45
Local Agents/Agents locaux
Librairie Payot, 6 rue Grenus, 1211 GENÈVE 11. Tel. 022.31.89.50
**TAIWAN – FORMOSE**
Good Faith Worldwide Int'l Co., Ltd.
9th floor, No. 118, Sec. 2
Chung Hsiao E. Road
TAIPEI. Tel. 391.7396/391.7397
**THAILAND – THAILANDE**
Suksit Siam Co., Ltd., 1715 Rama IV Rd,
Samyan, BANGKOK 5. Tel. 2511630
**TURKEY – TURQUIE**
Kültur Yayinlari Is-Türk Ltd. Sti.
Atatürk Bulvari No : 77/B
KIZILAY/ANKARA. Tel. 17 02 66
Dolmabahce Cad. No : 29
BESIKTAS/ISTANBUL. Tel. 60 71 88
**UNITED KINGDOM – ROYAUME-UNI**
H.M. Stationery Office, P.O.B. 569,
LONDON SE1 9NH. Tel. 01.928.6977, Ext. 410 or
49 High Holborn, LONDON WC1V 6 HB (personal callers)
Branches at: EDINBURGH, BIRMINGHAM, BRISTOL,
MANCHESTER, BELFAST.
**UNITED STATES OF AMERICA – ÉTATS-UNIS**
OECD Publications and Information Center, Suite 1207,
1750 Pennsylvania Ave., N.W. WASHINGTON, D.C.20006 – 4582
Tel. (202) 724.1857
**VENEZUELA**
Libreria del Este, Avda. F. Miranda 52, Edificio Galipan,
CARACAS 106. Tel. 32.23.01/33.26.04/33.24.73
**YUGOSLAVIA – YOUGOSLAVIE**
Jugoslovenska Knjiga, Terazije 27, P.O.B. 36, BEOGRAD.
Tel. 621.992

Les commandes provenant de pays où l'OCDE n'a pas encore désigné de dépositaire peuvent être adressées à :
OCDE, Bureau des Publications, 2, rue André-Pascal, 75775 PARIS CEDEX 16.
Orders and inquiries from countries where sales agents have not yet been appointed may be sent to:
OECD, Publications Office, 2 rue André-Pascal, 75775 PARIS CEDEX 16.

65958-12-1982

OECD PUBLICATIONS
2, rue André-Pascal
75775 PARIS CEDEX 16
No. 42435
(10 83 28 1) ISBN 92-64-12399-7
ISSN 0376-6438

●

*PRINTED IN FRANCE*